6 Radical Decisions

*How small groups of
Christ followers
can change the world,
through Kingdom Cells.*

Endorsements

"This is an awesome book describing a movement that will save the church from institutionalism and the world from an aloof and out of touch Christianity. The foundational emphases of Kingdom Cells result in a refocus on Christ, a transformed life and a Spirit empowered multiplication of mission teams that truly love one another. I would recommend we read this book and walk it out!"

Dr. Joel C. Hunter
Senior Pastor, Northland – A Church Distributed
Orlando, Florida, USA

"Matt Garvin calls us beyond the rhetoric of Christian theology to a radical commitment and missional obedience. These pages disclose a rare thoughtfulness in holding together a passion to see people come to faith and community transformation. A must read for fellow sojourners looking for 'a city with foundations, whose architect and builder is God.'"

Rev Moss Ntlha
General Secretary, The Evangelical Alliance of South Africa

"Matt Garvin has produced a challenging and very useful book. He has unerringly aimed at the core of Christian discipleship and effective mission and pointed a way to their renewal. If we could once more harness the power of 'Kingdom Cells' Christians would find themselves as a cutting edge movement again."

The Rev. Peter Corney OAM
Vicar emeritus St. Hilary's Anglican Church Kew, Melbourne, Australia
Founding director of the Australian Arrow Leadership Program

"6 Radical Decisions is a powerful, biblically rooted manifesto for changing the world. This simple picture of communities of people loving Christ and loving the world is beautifully illustrated with examples from church history and experiences from the Fusion movement. Garvin's infectious passion for authentic transformation spills onto the pages and is coupled with practical challenge. I will be re-reading this book with fellow dreamers and schemers, that we might see the Kingdom of God come in our locality!"

Andy Frost
Director of Share Jesus International

"In a deeply personal and passionate way, Matt draws together a wealth of distilled wisdom from the world's finest Christian leaders. This is a call for radical missional fellowship, through which we can – and must – impact the world for Christ."

Reverend Ruth Bushyager
Anglican Church, London

"We all need to hear it again fresh … you know, the clarion call. Pick up the thesaurus, thumb through, ah yes, there it is: 'Clarion call': 1. a direct public request for people to take action. Matt Garvin has enabled me to hear the call again, and issued with it direct request for action. This is not for the passive, but for those who are itching to live-out something radical and rich. It's a call to live a lifestyle of faith with Christ and others, messy and entwined yet potent. May we hear the clarion call together and start planning!"

Tania Bright
Deputy Director for Research and Development, The Salvation Army

"Matt Garvin has had an amazing journey for a young man and he has depth and vision beyond his years. His passion for every neighbourhood to have a living, loving, freedom-filled, wise action cell of Jesus followers to serve it, will grip you. His focus on spheres will be as divine guidance for many who are passionate to see change in society but, as yet, do not know how to be involved. His advocation of the legitimization of sodalities (action-focused communities) will transform pew-sitters who have been certain there is something more, but have been afraid to step out."

Tom Hallas
Field Director, Asia & Pacific, Youth with a Mission.

"6 Radical Decisions lays out a vision that can be lived out. It joins the dots of aspiration and engagement and puts a spring in the step of the Church."

Rich Wilson
National Team Leader, Fusion U.K.

"'…the Kingdom of God is at hand' were among the first words of Jesus and therefore reveal something very significant. Matt Garvin's book '6 Radical Decisions' is a very helpful book to enable God's people of all traditions to revisit the radical nature of Kingdom. I cannot help but think this may prove a resource that will help shape and inform the emerging mission communities, and fresh expression of Church."

Major Drew McCombe
Territorial Evangelism Secretary, Salvation Army, London

Endnote references are in the format:
Author of Publication, Title of Publication (Publication date), Page Number

Contents

This book is dedicated to

the remarkable people

of Fusion International

who strive to live

the 6 Radical Decisions

every day

Foreword

Are you tired of organisations and institutions?

Do you, like me, long for authentic movements? Movements that change the world, but are focused on their local community.

I first came across Fusion in South Africa in 2009, in the build up to the World Cup. They were there running their legendary "Open Crowd" Festivals. I saw them again in the Winter Olympics outreach in Vancouver. But I really got to know them and their heart in our work together for the More Than Gold mission across the UK for the 2012 Games.

I quickly realised that they are not about Festivals, but about "a group of mates that will do whatever it takes to reach their community." To be honest it sounds better with an Australian accent!

Matt Garvin, in this very profound book, quotes some of the greats as he eloquently navigates his way through Fusion's collective heart, mind and experiences. Page after page of wise words that I have found deeply helpful. I believe as Harry Truman challenges us, that Fusion wants to see Christians of all types accomplish great things and they don't care who gets the credit.

This book points the way forward by looking back to the original pattern of how God has worked in and through his children.

It's time for a new movement of God's people.
A movement that does what it says.

A movement that cares more about people than projects and programs.

A movement that believes God can use ordinary people to achieve extraordinary things.

A movement that can include all of us, that understands people and obeys God's call to local and global engagement.

This is book is not about the Fusion movement, this book is about our movement, a movement of Kingdom Cells working together to change the world.

I am so glad that God calls us to do mission on the 'rails of relationship', I don't want a lonely walk, I worry about those that do! I am so glad that God has allowed me to serve in relationship with my mates.

Together, is the cry - for God and our Community… Charge!

Jon Burns
UK Director, More than Gold;
Senior Pastor, CLV church, London; Founder and CEO, Lionsraw

Introduction

Why isn't the World Looking very Changed?

Our world is desperate. Everywhere I look people seem hungry for hope. People are longing for the wholeness and realness that can only come through Christ, yet we, the Christian church are not finding the ways to make the connection between the longing in their hearts and the truth of the gospel.

We Christians have been specifically charged with the responsibility of "seeking first his Kingdom and his righteousness."[1] We are invited to actively participate in seeing God's will happen here on earth in the same way it does in heaven.[2] We are called to harmonise with God in changing the world. This raises an obvious question: In a world that is roughly one third Christian[3], shouldn't things be looking a little different? *Why isn't the world looking very changed?*

Australian social researcher Richard Eckersley wrote: "There has never been a period in human history when so much hangs in the balance between what is and what might be, when so much depends on the choices we make as individuals, when it is so clear that we are, each of us, 'decision-makers' in deciding the destiny of humankind. And yet, because of the pressures, preoccupations and priorities of life today, we don't sense the significance of this moment—or sensing it, seem unable to hold it and be inspired by it. This is one of the most profound paradoxes of our times."[4]

One way, or another, the destiny of humankind is being decided at an increasingly rapid rate. We are in a moment of massive change, where the body of Christ has the chance, like never before, to change the world. But to do so we are going to need to face the truth that in order to change the world, it is we who must first change.

In Australian Rules Football, when a team is not going well, the coach will often say something like, "It's time we took a long hard look at ourselves." Perhaps as the Christian church it is time to take that long hard look at the disconnection between what we say we believe and what actually happens. We need to face the fact that some of the worst moments of the world's history, such as the Crusades, The Spanish inquisition, World War I, World War II, Apartheid and the Ku Klux Klan, all came out of nations that would call themselves Christian.

It's not just about nations either. In his book, *The Scandal of Evangelical Conscience*, Ronald J. Sider raises some concerning facts:[5]

- White evangelicals are the most likely people to object to neighbours of another race

- The richer Christians become, the less they give as a proportion of income

- If American Christians simply followed the biblical principle of tithing, it would be possible to deliver basic health care and education for <u>all</u> the poor on earth

- Divorce is more common among "born again" Christians than in the general American population

- 13% of traditional evangelicals say having extra marital sex is okay

- The percentage of Christian men involved in pornography is only marginally different to the rest of the world

- Theologically conservative Christians commit domestic abuse at least as often as the general public

Jesus indicated that it was our actions and not our words that distinguished us. He said "By their fruit you will recognize them."[6] I wonder what all of this fruit tells us? Sadly, perhaps Ghandi had a valid point when he said, "I like your Christ. I do not like your Christians. Your Christians are so unlike your Christ."[7]

A fairly convincing case can be put that not everyone who calls themselves Christian is acting within the will of God, which is the Kingdom of God. If N.T. Wright was correct that, "the gospel is the story of God's Kingdom being launched on earth as it is in heaven" and that, "We, as followers of Christ, have been both commissioned and equipped to put the victory over evil and God's new world into practise"[8] then perhaps we might need to explore how this actually happens.

While it is absolutely true that incredible damage has been done by people and nations who called themselves Christian, there is another side to the story. Time and time again, there have been moments over the last 2000 years that God has unequivocally used his people to bring his Kingdom and as a result, change the world. Small groups of Christ followers like Basil of Cappadocia, Saint Patrick, Count Zinzendorf, John Wesley, Hudson Taylor, Martin Luther-King and Mother Theresa have all brought light in the face of darkness, healing in the face of pain, and life in the face of death.

It is not only the great names of Christian history who have been used by God to bring His Kingdom. I have been privileged to travel to many parts of the world and to meet and work with many faithful people who love Jesus and are genuinely changing the world. In slums outside Jakarta, in a coloured community on the outskirts of Cape Town, in a fellowship of business people in Melbourne, in a village outside of Oxford, in an accommodation facility in Geraldton and in so many other places I have seen glimpses of what happens when the Kingdom of God comes on earth as it is in heaven.

As I reflected on what I was seeing around the world and what I read, I became more and more convinced that there is a common thread that runs through it all. Theologian Stanley Grenz asserts that the Kingdom of God consists in doing the will of God and that will always require a "radical decision."[9] I appreciate the way M. Scott Peck pointed out that: "The word 'radical' comes from the Latin *radix* meaning 'root' – the same word from which we get 'radish.'" He says "The proper radical is someone who tries to get to the root of things, not to be distracted by the superficials, to see the woods for the trees. It is good to be a radical. Anyone who thinks *deeply* will be one."[10]

Too often we put our trust in things like training, leadership, theology, and planning but we avoid the root of the problem because we don't make that radical decision to allow Jesus to be Lord. We separate our words from our actions. We fall into the trap of thinking Christianity is about ideas, and come up with plans to convince people of our ideas. Christian mission then becomes about selling ideas rather than the extension of the Kingdom of God.

The significant majority of Jesus' teaching came in the context of his action, as he explained what he was doing. When we accept a Christianity of ideas that is disconnected from the messiness of real life, we accept a Christianity that is disconnected from the Kingdom of God. I love Francis of Assisi's words, "It is no use walking anywhere to preach unless our walking is our preaching."[11]

Whenever God's Kingdom has been noticeably present, it has resulted in much more than people discovering a personal relationship with Christ, although that has always been fundamental. It has also transformed relationships, education, politics and economies. The Kingdom of God is about every area of life.

This book is an attempt to get to the root of what it actually means to take Jesus' charge seriously to "seek first his kingdom and his righteousness."[12] As Stanley Grenz says, to do so is a "radical decision." I am using the term *Kingdom Cell* to describe a group of people who have made one big radical decision: to accept Jesus Christ as king, which has led to five other decisions. The decisions are not complicated but they are certainly life changing.

I am conscious that the term "cell" was used through the 1970's and 80's to describe church small groups or fellowship groups (Cell groups). I am also conscious that most recently the term has also been used in relationship to terrorists (terrorist Cells). A Kingdom Cell is quite different from the original idea of church cell groups and is the exact opposite of terrorist cells. The reason that the word is the right one to describe the central idea of this book though, is that cells are the fundamental units of life. All living organisms are composed of, and dependent on cells to function normally. Cells (usually) have a nucleus that contains their life and cells are the core agents of biological growth. All of these characteristics are true of Kingdom Cells. As cells are to the human body, Kingdom Cells are to the body of Christ.

The first chapter of the book will explore the relationship between Kingdom Cells and the body of Christ, but then the book will get more personal. The Kingdom of God is not an abstract concept, it asks deeply confronting questions of each one of us, about the decisions by which we live our lives. It is with those questions we must wrestle if we are to see the life of a Kingdom Cell. By the end of this book, I hope you will be left with a sense of hope, but also a sense of purpose. The world needs Christianity that is not off with the fairies or up with the elites, but is at home in the complexity, the pain and the messiness of real life.

The 6 Radical Decisions of the Kingdom Cell:

1. The decision that Jesus is Lord
2. The decision to accept a mission
3. The decision to be in fellowship
4. The decision to be hospitable
5. The decision to empower
6. The decision to commit

The world is hungry for the lived faith of the Kingdom Cell that time and again over the last 2000 years has transformed cities and nations, and now provides a way forward for the church in the 21st Century.

1

The *Other* Structure
of the Body of Christ

I need my local church. In the community of my local congregation I take off whatever hat I may wear in the world and I come as an equal with other brothers and sisters of all ages to reaffirm my love for Jesus. It is here every week that I am reminded of his love for me, and it is here that each week I am invited to recommit my life to him.

There seems to be an increasing number of people who are moving towards a personalisation of faith and away from commitment to a local congregation. They are missing something important. I am also concerned about those people who find such deep fellowship in a mission group that they neglect membership of the local church. Not being actively committed to a local congregation leads to the loss of some of the critical foundations of Christian discipleship.

Even for those who still regularly attend a Sunday service, we can fall into the trap of seeing it as a performance for which we are the audience, and when the performance is no longer what we prefer we start to shop around for something that might suit us better. This consumer approach to church robs us of the richness that fellowship in the body of Christ is meant to be.

As we come together, in fellowship, to worship Christ, we are given a renewed sense of perspective we can gain no other way. We need communion and baptism, we need Bible teaching, we need worship, and we need communal prayer to help us keep our focus where it needs to be: on Christ. It is in this setting of broad fellowship in the context of worship, the word and sacraments that we are reminded that we, and our mission, are not the centre of the universe.

We also need the fellowship we find only in a local congregation, with our brothers and sisters of different ages, from different backgrounds and with different skills. It is precisely the differences that make the body of Christ what it is. It was this truth that Paul was addressing with the imagery of the body in 1 Corinthians 12. We need a place where we know others will share the load of our burdens, and where we will learn to share the burdens of others as Paul encourages us to.[13] It is not an accident that the great chapter on love (1 Corinthians 13) comes after the chapter in which Paul makes clear the importance of individuality in the body of Christ. We need the diversity of the body of Christ in order to discover what it truly means to love.

In his book *Christ Plays in Ten Thousand places*, Eugene Peterson argues that there is a real danger of our vocation becoming our identity, and our identity replacing God without the rhythm of Sabbath: "If there is no Sabbath – no regular and commanded not-working, not-talking – we soon become totally absorbed in what we are doing and saying, and God's work is either forgotten or marginalised. When we work we are most god-like, which means that it is in our work that it is easiest to develop god-pretensions. Un-sabbathed, our work becomes the entire context in which we define our lives. We lose the capacity to sing, "This is my Father's world" and end up chirping little self-centred ditties about what we are doing and feeling."[14]

One of the most respected theologians of the twentieth century, Karl Barth, pointed out just how central the local congregation is to the body of Christ when he wrote "The Church lives (she is) in this visible, concrete transaction (prayer, confession of faith, Baptism, Lord's Supper, the proclamation and reception of the Gospel) and in its presuppositions (theology, training of the young) and its consequences (brotherly discipline, pastoral care and other oversight). The Church lives (she actually is) in the form of a local congregation, which is the basis of all other forms of her life."[15]

Many books have been published about how to "do church" in a bigger, healthier or more missional way, and many models from successful churches have been studied and copied. So far this conversation has been largely focused on the shape and form of the local congregation. Because the congregation is so important, it is understandable that so much energy is put into it, however as Barth points out, there are also "other forms of her life."

In focussing primarily on the congregation, and losing sight of the other forms of life, we have reduced our understanding of what it means to be the body of Christ. Mark Greene, the executive director of the *London Institute for Contemporary Christianity*, wrote an essay called *The Great Divide* in which he argues that the church has fallen into the trap of separating sacred and secular, and as a result we are failing in our mission because we are not helping our people discover that they have a ministry that extends beyond the borders of the Sunday service or midweek small group.

He says "It is because of SSD (Sacred Secular Divide) that the vast majority of Christians feel that they do not get any significant support for their daily work from the teaching, preaching, prayer, worship, pastoral, group aspects of local church life. No support for how they spend fifty percent of their waking lives."[16] Mark quotes one teacher as saying "I spend an hour a week teaching Sunday school and they haul me up in front of the church to pray for me. The rest of the week I'm a full time teacher and the church has never prayed for me. That says it all."[17]

More and more people are finding their ministry outside the context of the Sunday service or mid-week small groups. There is a move amongst business people to recognize that their work is their ministry. I am seeing the same thing amongst artists, health care professionals, politicians, mothers, builders, youth workers and rock and roll musicians. As I engage with lots of different church structures and lots of different believers and non-believers, it seems clear that God is up to something far bigger than simply reorganising the church. Respected theologian, John Howard Yoder, believed that the church is still waiting for the "Reformation that has yet to happen," which will be about the discovery that *every member of the body of Christ has a ministry.*[18]

This does not at all invalidate the vital call for some to minister to, within and on behalf of the local church; it just means we need to understand that the job of the congregation is not to get more people into the congregation; it is to get more of the congregation out into the world. Ephesians 4:11-13 makes it clear that some people are called to the specific ministry of building up the body of Christ towards maturity.

The *Apostle* was to live on the frontiers, bringing the Kingdom to new places in new and unexpected ways. In their wake they left fledgling groups of Christians who were bringing the Kingdom of God into their particular context. The *Prophet* was to speak God's word into this moment, not only to the church but also to the world. It was their job to highlight the places of darkness where the Kingdom of God was still to permeate. The *Evangelist* had the joyful task of inviting people into God's Kingdom by introducing them to Jesus. The *Pastor/Teachers*[19] were to carry the weight of responsibility for those in their care. They were to walk alongside their flock, loving them, helping them discover their vocation, and equipping them to fulfil it. These gifts are still sorely needed in the church today. However, our paradigm of church has reduced their effectiveness and missed the whole point of what Paul was trying to communicate.

Paul says the purpose of the gifts was to "Equip his people for works of service, so that the body of Christ may be built up until we all reach unity in the faith and in the knowledge of the Son of God and become mature, attaining to the whole measure of the fullness of Christ."[20] The purpose of the Apostle, Prophet, Evangelist and Pastor/Teacher was to release the body of Christ into the world as mature disciples of Jesus.

As increasingly we discover that our ministry and mission is not just in the context of the church, we need to rediscover the structures that enable us to fulfil our call as missionaries and ministers to the world. Missiologist Ralph Winter believed[21] that throughout the history of the church God has used two primary structures in the body of Christ. The first structure was **the congregation**, which Winter gave the technical title modality. He said that the "defining characteristic of this structure is that it includes old and young, male and female."[22] The second structure was **the missionary band**, which Winter gave the technical title of *sodality*. He said that this grouping of people were committed, experienced and aligned themselves with a "second decision beyond membership in the first structure."[23] While there is, and needs to be, a place for everyone in the congregation, only those who have committed to the mission can find a place in a missionary band. Winter contrasted the small group of friends that surrounded Paul and Barnabas, to the church in Antioch to describe the difference between the congregation and the missionary band. He points out that Paul and Barnabas had a mission that was clearly beyond the context of the church, and that they had made a "second decision" on top of their commitment to Christ, in order to commit to that mission.

While Ralph Winter was primarily focussed on a traditional view of mission, and would have seen that those in missionary bands were different to those in the congregation, I believe his insight is extremely helpful in seeing that we might need more than one structure if we are to bridge the Sacred-Secular divide. If we accept as John Howard Yoder believes, that the Christian Church is on a journey to discover that we all have a ministry, and that for many of us that ministry will be beyond the context of our local congregation, then I would like to suggest that we need to re-discover the importance of missionary bands as another structure in the body of Christ.

This is not a new idea, and as I will unpack in the following chapters of the book, throughout the last 2000 years, whenever the church has been at its best, there have always been these small groups that set the culture and tone through their love for Jesus and commitment to a mission that was about making the values of the Kingdom of God manifest in their particular context. I call these missionary bands, *Kingdom Cells*, which I have come to see, are the result of 6 radical decisions.

We need the local congregation. We need the worship and the kind of fellowship with people committed to different ministries, and even people not committed to any ministry, that only the congregation can provide, but at the same time we need more. If we are ready to answer the specific call of God on our lives, we will do it most effectively as part of a Kingdom Cell. We need other brothers and sisters who love Jesus, are committed to the same mission that we are, love each other, are ready to be hospitable and will empower those they connect with to become themselves. We need both these structures of the body of Christ if we are to truly seek first the Kingdom of God.

2

The Journey of Discovery

Fusion started as the dream of one teenager, and over the course of fifty years grew to become an international movement. My dad, Mal, was the founder of Fusion Australia.[24] Like many Christian organisations, Fusion started with a simple commitment to share the gospel with teenagers, a commitment which is still at its heart today.

As Mal and the team started to connect with those who responded, Fusion found itself with one foot in the complex world of young people, their families and communities, and one foot in the church. It was from this place that Fusion began a process of trial, error, reflection and learning that meant they were continually refining their action and their understanding.

Faced with the issues confronting the young people they worked with, Fusion started to speak out about issues of justice. Mal developed a nationally syndicated radio program and the organisation published a youth magazine. Fusion also established some of Australia's first refuges for homeless young people, youth drop-in centres and youth cafes. The organisation also intentionally fostered creativity and the arts.

Fusion found a particular role in helping churches work together in mission. They helped coordinate one of the biggest prayer meetings in Australia's history in 1988 (50,000 people gathered on the steps of New Parliament

House), and the biggest coordinated action by Christians in the Nation's history (the 1994 Global March for Jesus, where over 250,000 took part).

Throughout this journey, Fusion kept learning, and developed training programs and resources that encapsulated what God had been showing them. While many people think and read their way to theology, the people of Fusion lived their way to a very practical theology of the Kingdom of God that was also a philosophy of action.

As I write this, I am in the process of transitioning out of leadership in Fusion, however I will always love the people, the values and the big dream that make the organisation unique. Serving with Fusion for twenty years has given me the unique opportunity to be friends both with street kids and with bishops, to hang out with artists and with business people, to teach large groups of Christian leaders and play with children in Indonesian slums.

Working with Fusion has given me an opportunity to engage with the breadth of the Christian church in so many parts of the world. This unique perspective has had a significant influence on this book; however the basis for this book actually started as a personal crisis.

I still remember the meeting when I was invited to move to the Australian state of Victoria. Fusion's work in Victoria had imploded. All the leaders had left and there was a small team left wondering whether they had a future.

I had arrived in Tasmania, twelve years earlier, to work with Fusion as an idealistic and naïve 20 year old and was preparing to leave having learned a great deal, loving the place and the people, but feeling burned out. I really didn't want to think about what Victoria would mean. As I went home and spoke to my wife Leeanne, we both knew however, that it was the right option. As we prayed and talked, that conviction only got stronger.

As I reached for a way to make sense of the job, I knew there were some things I could say with integrity:

-       Fusion is not always at its best, but when it is, it is remarkable.
-       When we are at our best we love Jesus.

- When we are at our best we are deeply connected to the communities we are in and are actively working to serve them.
- When we are at our best we build a sense of community from the core of our teams.
- When we are at our best we are part of a big dream of seeing the whole world transformed as part of a national and international movement.

So as I put it all together I came up with a sentence that I just said over and over again: *When Fusion is at its best we love our communities, love each other and are part of a National and International fellowship because we love Jesus.* It wasn't particularly poetic, or even very clever, but it was a picture of what we were meant to be that I believed in deeply and that gave me a bearing as I went into Victoria. I'm sure the team got sick of me saying that one sentence, but it not only gave me my direction, it gave us our goal, and the ministry in Victoria grew significantly.

It was five years later that I started to see the broader implications of what I glimpsed in Victoria. At that time I was adjusting to the idea that I, along with three others, were now leading the Fusion movement internationally following my Father's retirement. As I sat on a long haul flight to Canada, I was wrestling with how I could prepare the leadership team there to lead Christians into mission for the 2010 Winter Games. One of the dilemmas of outreach at big events is that so often nothing is left after all the energy and activity.

I read through old Fusion plans and publications and I started to see a pattern emerge. I had been reading a number of books on Church history and teaching about different moments when the Christian church exploded. As I thought about those heroes of the past, a pattern came into focus. I started to see a strong similarity between the things I had seen in Fusion and other Christian ministries when they were at their best, and the things that have brought the church to life over the last 2000 years. As I reflected, I realised that the same things were true of me when I was at my best, too.

I started to scribble a diagram on my legal pad. While the circles and lines were not neat and tidy, the truth they captured was both simple and powerful. I came to a point where I realised that what I was writing and drawing was no longer just representing the story of one organisation, but really the Christian church, when it is at its best. What I had captured was not so much a vision or a plan but a life, or more accurately a description of the factors that contribute to that life.

It became abundantly clear that this world has been, and will be changed, by people who simply:

1. Love Jesus and are motivated by that love
2. Commit themselves to a mission
3. Are in fellowship
4. Are hospitable
5. Empower others
6. Are committed

As I looked around Fusion and recalled my reading of church history I saw that when these decisions were made and congruent with the Kingdom of God, life naturally was created. I also saw how often groups or churches get one or two of these things right but miss the others. I could see for instance how Fusion teams are often very committed to a mission and are continually striving for fellowship but the focus on Jesus can easily go missing. I could see how for many of my friends the focus on personal faith was strong but there was no real long-term commitment to anything beyond themselves.

As I started to share the diagram with others, both they and I started to get excited. It was simple, but it captured something important. With all its circles, arrows and lines, it helped me see what my heart had been telling me for a long time: effectiveness in mission and ministry is not about what we do, it's about who we are.

The Kingdom Cell is not an attempt to create a new theory or a new way of doing things. It is simply an attempt to describe what has happened, and does happen, when God is free to engage the world through his people.

The Kingdom Cell Diagram

The Kingdom Cell diagram is what I scribbled on my legal pad on the way to Canada.

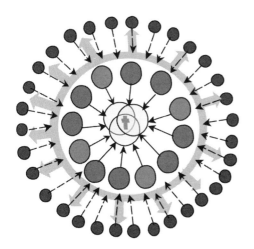

At the centre of the diagram is the cross of Christ, representing the fact that everything of value comes from Him.

Surrounding the central circles is a large circle with arrows pointing outwards, symbolizing that Christian vocation is found in bringing Christ to the world.

At the core of the Kingdom Cell are three overlapping circles, which represent the deep fellowship of those who have given their lives to Jesus, for a mission.

On the outside of the big circle are lots of little circles with dotted arrows pointing inward. This represents the fact that a Kingdom Cell is attractive, and that the life produced between people who love Jesus, who are committed to a mission and who love each other, will result in people wanting to connect.

On the inside of the big circle are circles of two different shades, representing those who have joined the mission of the Kingdom Cell, and are being empowered as they move towards the centre, who is Christ.

These people are attracted inwards to the heart of the Cell and are being empowered by the Cell to find their own vocation in Christ.

This book is an attempt to unpack the six radical decisions represented by this diagram, and as the book unfolds, the meaning behind each element will be brought into focus.

3

The First Radical Decision: Jesus

The young Anglican priest boarded the boat home from America to England in a cloud of depression. Everything he had learned in theological college had failed him. The career path that once seemed so sure was now surely a dead end. The young man described his faith this way: "I was strongly convinced that the cause of that uneasiness was unbelief, and that gaining a true, living faith was the one thing needful for me. But still I fixt not this faith on its right object: I meant only faith in God, not faith in or through Christ." [25]

In the middle of the Atlantic sea, the boat hit a violent storm. As if having all his dreams shattered wasn't enough, the young man faced the very real prospect of his life coming to an end in a watery grave. As he leaned over the side of the boat vomiting for the fourth time, he heard a sound that was both strangely comforting and yet profoundly out of place in such a fear filled moment.

He heard people singing hymns in a way he hadn't heard people sing hymns ever before. It was as if the music was coming from deep inside of them. It was as if they believed deeply every word that came out of their mouths. They were an oasis of peace in the midst of the chaos.

John Wesley was deeply impacted by what he heard and found himself attracted to this group of believers, the Moravians, who seemed so different from him. After arriving in London, the believers he had met on the boat invited him to a Bible study that would change not only his life, but also the course of English history. Wesley describes the event in his own words: "In the evening I went very unwillingly to a society in Aldersgate Street, where one was reading Luther's preface to the Epistle to the Romans. About a quarter before nine, while he was describing the change which God works in the heart through faith in Christ, I felt my heart strangely warmed. I felt that I did trust in Christ, Christ alone for salvation, and an assurance was given me, that he had taken away my sins, even MINE, and saved ME from the law of sin and death."[26]

So John Wesley moved from a commitment to an unknown God who was "out there", to a personal relationship with Jesus Christ. This shift was so personally profound that it called into question his whole approach to ministry to that point. Wesley, following the example of George Whitefield,[27] moved out of the church buildings and into the streets and fields. He not only led thousands to a personal relationship with Christ, he trained 541 itinerant preachers, wrote extensively on everything from the bible to personal hygiene and spoke out about issues of social justice, including slavery. John Wesley was the catalyst for a major revival of Christianity across the United Kingdom. Wesley did not want to start another Christian denomination and died as an Anglican, however today around the world around 70,000,000 people call themselves Methodists.[28] In 2002, a BBC poll named Wesley as the 50th (out of 100) greatest Briton of all time.[29] All of this came from a personal encounter with Jesus Christ.

Jesus isn't a program, an idea or even a feeling. Jesus is a person. Only a living, open, free relationship with him, and submission to his will, produces the kind of life that fuels a Kingdom Cell. Over the years, one of the things I have found most precious about Fusion is the deep commitment the organisation and its people have to the ministry of reconciliation that it adopted as its mandate from 2 Corinthians 5:17-21. One of things I see both in Fusion and in myself, however, is the very real danger that we can end up as activists, focused on what we do. I see the same danger in most people deeply committed to a job, ministry or mission.

It took me a while to realise that Paul had probably seen the same tendency, which he tried to address a couple of verses earlier in 2 Corinthians 5:14: *"For Christ's love compels us, because we are convinced that one died for all, and therefore all died."* In the Greek this passage could mean either Christ's love for us compels us, or our love for Christ compels us. They are both true.

The more I can really believe that Jesus loves me, as I am, without having to do anything to deserve that love, the less I will be driven by the other voices inside me that tell me what I need to do or be in order to be "okay". The more I can know and love Jesus, with integrity, from my heart, the freer I will be to be myself.

Grace means that there is absolutely nothing we need to do for Jesus to love us. Grace is something we receive. Jesus is constantly with us, reaching out a hand to welcome us into deeper relationship. However, a relationship requires two people. There is simply no substitute for time with another person in a relationship. No matter how close you might be, time away from each other means that a relationship moves apart.

Author Don Miller in *Blue Like Jazz* recounts a story of a man named Alan who went around the country asking ministry leaders questions. "It sounded very boring except for one visit he made to a man named Bill Bright, the president of a big ministry. Alan said he was a big man, full of life who listened without shifting his eyes. Alan asked a few questions. I don't know what they were, but as a final question he asked Dr. Bright what Jesus meant to him. Alan said Dr. Bright could not answer the question. He said Dr. Bright just started to cry. He sat there in his big chair behind his big desk and wept."[30]

Even as I write this, I feel personally challenged. I can get so busy about Christian work, or simply about stuff that feels good, that the face of Jesus gets obscured. I know that for me, the choice to relate to Jesus is actually a daily one (in all honesty it's probably a minute by minute one). Only by living in this wrestle of faith, by being in a place where I can actually talk about God's love as a personal experience and not simply a theological concept, will the life of Jesus be free to move at the centre of a Kingdom Cell. The starting point of transformation is not actually thinking about mission, church, theology or anything else. The starting point and anchor for any true Kingdom work, is a living and active love for the person of Jesus Christ. Almost nothing else matters.

Commitment to Jesus means commitment to a relationship. An important starting place for me personally was developing the habit of creating the space each day for time with Jesus. I can't see how a mature faith can develop without space for prayer and reflection on the Word of God. This daily re-orientation to the fact that there is a God and he loves me has been one of my life-lines in moments where things feel overwhelming. Commitment to Jesus also means commitment to his body on earth, the church. Corporate worship and the sacraments are another essential part of regular re-orientation for me.

If the person of Jesus is not at the core of what we do, anything else we might try in the name of faith is a waste of time. Mother Theresa summed it up when she said: *"Many people mistake our work for our vocation. Our vocation is the love of Jesus."*[31]

Unless you are in a real relationship with Jesus, unless you are prepared to give your life in service to Christ the King, the rest of this book is a waste of time. Jesus loves you, and ultimately the only thing of any value you can actually do is love him in return. Nothing matters more than that.

If you look at all the significant movements of God's spirit in the last 2000 years you will find at their heart people who discovered Jesus Christ in the same way that John Wesley did, and made a commitment to a relationship with Him. Alan Hirsch in his book "Forgotten Ways" says: "I have become absolutely convinced that it is Christology, and in particular the primitive, unencumbered Christology of the NT church, that lies at the heart of the renewal of the church at all times and in every age."[32]

St. Patrick laid the foundations for the Celtic church, which eventually became a little beacon of light through the blackness and corruption of the Middle Ages. A short prayer known as St. Patrick's Breastplate makes it clear where the source of his energy and ministry lay:

Christ be with me, Christ within me,
Christ behind me, Christ before me,
Christ beside me, Christ to win me,
Christ to comfort and restore me,
Christ beneath me, Christ above me,
Christ in quiet, Christ in danger,
Christ in hearts of all that love me,
Christ in mouth of friend and stranger.

At the core of a Kingdom Cell are those who have had a personally transforming encounter with Jesus Christ. They are people who are living from the solid foundation of that relationship in their everyday lives and because of that foundation have discovered a mission and a vocation to bring the life of Christ to a hurting world.

Author and speaker, Priscilla Shirer, captured something important when she said, "In the first century in Palestine, Christianity was a community of believers. Then Christianity moved to Greece and became a philosophy. Then it moved to Rome and became an institution. Then it moved to Europe and became a culture. And then it moved to America and became a business. We need to get back to being a healthy, vibrant community of true followers of Jesus."[33]

A fresh understanding of <u>real</u> Christianity

Jesus himself described why, for many people, the Kingdom of God would not become a lived reality. In the parable of the sower, he described four general responses people would have to the Kingdom. The first group he talks about simply won't hear. The truth will never penetrate their consciousness. The second group would hear and have a significant emotional response but would not allow themselves to face the deeper issues. When the going gets tough, they get going. The third group both hear and understand the implications of the Kingdom of God, but the agenda of the world would become their priority as things like relationships, jobs and money would get in the way. Only the fourth group hear, understand and live out the truth of the Kingdom of God.[34] I think most of us, if we were honest, can see ourselves in all four of the groups Jesus identifies.

The Kingdom of God is confronting because there is no way to master it, it is about submission to a master. We are only enabled to make the radical choice to *seek first the Kingdom of God* only to the extent we are open to, and led by, the Spirit of God.

N.T. Wright asserts that "I have sometimes heard Christian people talk as though, having done what he's done in Jesus, God now wants us to do our part by getting on with things under our own steam. But that is a tragic misunderstanding. It leads either to arrogance or burnout, or both. Without God's Spirit, there is nothing we can do that will count for God's Kingdom. Without God's Spirit, the church simply can't be the church."[35]

Jesus says, "I am the way and the truth and the life. No one comes to the Father except through me."[36] This statement is unequivocal, yet so often we equivocate. This is a book about Kingdom Cells, but you cannot have a Kingdom without a King. A mascot or a best buddy might feel safer, but you can't have half a relationship with Jesus. It's all or nothing.

In biological terms, Jesus would be like the D.N.A. of a Kingdom Cell. Without a nucleus of people acting out of a mature relationship of love with Jesus, any outreach program we try to run, any church we try to plant, in fact anything we try to do for the sake of the Kingdom of God, will be a waste of time. With a real, personal relationship with Jesus, however, anything is possible!

4

The Second Radical Decision: a Mission

For many years we in the church have been seeing mission primarily as about conversion to the Christian faith. This was a natural result of the way we thought through the 19th and 20th centuries, where the underlying assumption was that ultimately human understanding would solve every problem. It was in this era that we came up with the "isms" that caused so much conflict in the world: communism, capitalism, atheism, conservatism, existentialism, Gnosticism, individualism, liberalism, nihilism, perfectionism, pessimism, socialism, spiritualism, subjectivism and fundamentalism (to name just a few).[37] We fell into the trap of thinking Christianity was just another "ism" that had to fight for space with all the others. In the 21st century most of us have worked out that none of the "isms" have all the truth and some have very little.

As we find ourselves in what a lot of people call a 'post-modern' world (really a post "ism" world), I want to suggest that seeing mission as selling the Christian idea is too small. We each have a mission to fulfil in God's grand plan. From Jesus' first recorded words, "Did you not know that I must be about my Father's business?", to some of his last before the cross, "I have brought you glory on earth by finishing the work you gave me to do" it is clear that Jesus was acutely aware of his God given mission. We too need to become aware of ours.

Ephesians 2:10 says, "For we are God's handiwork, created in Christ Jesus to do good works, which God prepared in advance for us to do." Each one of us is on a lifelong journey to become who God intended us to be, through living out God's call on our lives. N.T. Wright points out, "One of the great triumphs of the movie *The Lord of the Rings* is that it … (urges) us to find our true selves by following and staying loyal to the vocation that we wouldn't have chosen, that comes to us from outside."[38]

The purpose of our lives is not something we invent, nor is it something we discover by listening to our feelings. Author and concentration camp survivor, Victor Frankl said, "We detect rather than invent our missions in life. Everyone has his own specific vocation or mission in life, therein he cannot be replaced, nor can his life be repeated. Thus, everyone's task is unique as is his specific opportunity to implement it."[39]

This is as true for those we work with as it is for us. As God brings people, our job is not to plug them into whatever gap might be most pressing, or even what job they asked for, but to take the time to understand why God brought them in the first place. Just because someone has a particular skill might not mean it is right for them to do a particular job, even if it is a crying need. The question for each of us is not what can we do, but what the mission is that God is inviting us to. Simon Walker says, "A leader enables others to identify and embrace their own vocations. This is not career guidance. This is more than identifying some passion or drive or skill that might suit a particular job or role. This is helping someone else to come to understand what their unique and specific calling in the world may involve."[40]

I learned the importance of mission by watching my father, Mal, working on his mission and later in reading church history I saw the pattern for myself. My dad grew up outside the church, on the streets of Sydney's suburbs. His father died when he was three, and despite his mother remarrying, the family never fully recovered. Dad speaks of two people who were crucial to how he would eventually turn out: a grandmother who saw and loved him, and a secondary school teacher who saw and challenged him. Apart from that one teacher, he didn't enjoy school and took the first opportunity available to him to leave, taking a job as an apprentice manufacturing jeweller.

He looks back fondly on his days in the workshop and enjoys relating some of the practical jokes he and others would play on unsuspecting new apprentices. One day, one of those apprentices, Kevin (who earned the nickname 'Greased Lightning' because he was slow at everything) invited Mal to a Christian Easter camp. Initially looking for a polite excuse to say 'no', Mal changed his mind after Kevin pointed out that there would be attractive girls there.

Arriving at the camp, the fifteen year old from Mortlake felt like a fish out of water. To make matters worse Kevin decided at the last minute not to come. As the campers sat down to the evening meal, Mal began to tuck into the food eagerly before he realised no one else was eating. Almost spontaneously the whole group burst into a nursery-rhyme-like song that Mal had never heard before and an anxious knot appeared in his stomach.

That night as he prepared for bed he noticed one of the young campers sitting lotus style on the floor reading his Bible. When he woke up, the boy was still there, giving no indication that he had even been to bed. Mal started to concoct reasons to leave, but couldn't find one that seemed like it would hold water. Thankfully one of the camp leaders, Ron, spotted the hapless young man, who stood out like a sore thumb as he tried to mouth the words to the songs everyone else seemed to know by heart. Ron caught up with Mal later that day as he was retreating to his dorm room. "Mal, are you a Christian?" he asked. Thinking quickly and remembering the boys down the street had dressed up in funny white clothes for something called confirmation, Mal replied, "Ah no Ron, but I'm expecting to get done next month." Ron smiled and asked whether he would be interested in understanding more from the Bible about what a Christian was.

As Ron began to explain the truth of the gospel, Mal recalls, "A profound response rose in my heart and in floods of tears I asked Jesus into my heart. And he came in. I certainly wasn't an instant saint and have never been a "religious" person, but that transaction explains the next fifty years of my life."[41]

On that Good Friday evening, Mal discovered a Father who wouldn't leave him. He wanted to know why it had taken this long for someone to let him in on the news and immediately he wanted to tell all of his friends. He bowled up to the local Anglican minister with plans for a rock and roll concert where people like him could hear about Jesus. The curt response, "Malcolm, don't you know that God could never use the music of the dance floor?" just didn't ring true to the teenager who was now on a mission.

He and his friends started organizing outings that were really just excuses to share the gospel. "On the first trip only one of the young people had the courage not to become a Christian. We were very enthusiastic but not very aware." The more Mal got to know Jesus, the more he wanted other young people to discover what he had found. He told me, "I wanted to give my life so that other young people like me could know Jesus, so I began to pray. I imagined my life was a cheque. I told Jesus that I would be willing to pay any price he asked of me so that people like me could know Him. Each day I prayed the same prayer, and each day more of me prayed it. At the end of a week praying the same prayer, something happened. I sensed God connected with me in a special way and took me up on the offer. From that point on I knew what the job was." Mal had accepted a mission.

That heart commitment to seeing young people know Jesus in a real way became the impetus for a movement which has now has spread around the world. In all the Christian history and testimonies I've read subsequently, I've discovered that almost everyone who has been used by God has been through a similar sort of transaction with Him. There is a moment where you accept the burden of responsibility, where you choose to accept your unique mission, and that moment changes everything. Before you choose a mission, you need others for a sense of direction. After you choose, you are free to throw out the old game plan because you are playing a new game.

Becoming yourself

Charlotte Perkins Gilman said, "The first duty of a human being is to assume the right functional relationship to society - more briefly, to find your real job, and do it."[42] It is right, for a period of all our lives to be about becoming us. The primary vocation for a child is to enjoy the life God has given them and to take the complex journey of discovery that is adolescence. At some point though, we will be confronted with the life defining question, *"What am I here for?"*

A baby genuinely believes that its mother is an extension of itself. When it cries it expects its mother to fix the problem. The bond between a mother and a baby is a beautiful thing but as the baby grows into a child and the child grows into an adult, a separation must happen if the baby is to be a healthy human being. This journey of separation is not an easy one, and sometimes parents who don't want to face the grief of letting go, encourage their children to stay dependant on them.

It is normal for adolescents, and even adults to deeply fear being seen as 'different'. We desperately want to 'fit in'. Acceptance matters deeply, and all of us can bring to mind painful moments when that acceptance we so desperately wanted just wasn't there. Gradually, all being well, we start to discover that spending our lives looking for the acceptance of others will never ultimately lead to fulfilment. Whenever we avoid difficult conversations because people may react badly, or we say things we don't believe in order to get people to like us, there is part of us that knows we are selling ourselves short. We start to discover that we are different and we then begin a lifelong journey to know, and gradually accept ourselves. This journey lasts a lifetime, and many people get stuck along the way.

The writer of Hebrews contrasts mature and immature Christians by saying in 5:13 and 14, "Anyone who lives on milk, being still an infant, is not acquainted with the teaching about righteousness. But solid food is for the mature, who by constant use have trained themselves to distinguish good from evil."

So the writer of Hebrews is defining the immature as those who continue to need someone to hold their hand and patiently explain their relationship to God, themselves and the world. Paul gives a picture of immaturity in Ephesians 4 where he talks about "infants tossed back and forth by waves." Again in this picture we see how an immature person needs external support in order to maintain a right relationship to God, themselves and the world.

It is clear that the writers of the New Testament believed it was possible to develop a mature faith that gave a foundation for life. It is right for a baby to be immature, to need the external support of its parents in order to live, but that baby must eventually grow up. A mother hasn't finished her work until her once helpless baby no longer needs her. The main task for a child is to become a mature adult and to become truly themselves. Sadly, too many adults are still travelling the identity-seeking journey of children. One of the saddest things I have seen is when a 40 year old still acts like a self-centred teenager.

Eugene Petersen captures this truth in his paraphrase[43] of 1 Peter 1:14-17: "Don't lazily slip back into those old grooves of evil, doing just what you feel like doing. You didn't know any better then; you do now. As obedient children, let yourselves be pulled into a way of life shaped by God's life, a life energetic and blazing with holiness."

As we centre ourselves on Him, being willing to give up our lives to Him, then we start to actually discover our lives. We move towards maturity, becoming more and more whole-hearted as we discover that righteousness is not living by a set of rules but moving into right relationship with God, our world and ourselves. We become more and more free.

C.S. Lewis said, "The more we let God take us over, the more truly ourselves we become - because he made us. He invented all the different people that you and I were intended to be ... It is when I turn to Christ, when I give up myself to his personality, that I first begin to have a real personality of my own."[44]

Two of the things that make a big difference in the journey towards maturity are a love for Christ and the acceptance of a personal mission. Both of these choices call us beyond ourselves and in just the way Jesus said would happen,[45] as we willingly let go of our own agendas, we actually discover our true selves.

A mature person is someone who has a fairly accurate picture of themselves, and has come to terms with the fact that they are different from others. Bestselling author, Stephen Covey followed up his massively successful 7 Habits of Highly Successful People, a number of years later with The 8th Habit. Covey defined the eighth habit as 'finding your voice and helping others to find theirs.' He had realised that it was one thing to be effective; it was another thing entirely, to be yourself.

Paul wrote to the Galatians that "each one should carry his own load." The Greek word here for load is *phortion* means the pack carried by a marching soldier. While there are some loads we need our brothers and sisters in Christ to carry with us, we each have the particular burden which we are individually called to bear. Your load is the mission to which God has called you as well as the daily battle with yourself. The more you open yourself to Jesus, the more you will have to face the parts of you that don't want to. The more you commit to a mission, the more a part of you will scream out for an easier way. No-one else can carry these loads for you.

2 Corinthians 5:17 says "Therefore, if anyone is in Christ, the new creation has come: The old has gone, the new is here!" The Greek word for *new creation* is *Ktisis*. That word more literally means a blueprint, and not a finished product. What Paul is actually saying is something like, "If you have invited Jesus to come in as Lord of your life, you have commenced a project with him to build your life. He has the plans, so make sure you stay in touch with the architect!" Each one of us has a God-given mission that might change or develop as we go on, but is always intimately tied up with God's redemptive work of bringing his Kingdom to earth.

I was grateful that Shane Claiborne pointed out that Matthew 11:29-30 should actually read, "Come to me, all you who are weary and burdened and I will give you rest. Take my yoke upon you and learn from me, for I am gentle and humble in heart, and you will find rest for your souls. For my yoke is good and my burden light." Unfortunately many English versions of the bible translate the Greek word *chrestos* which means good or well fitting as easy. The path of seeking first the Kingdom is the way to maturity, it is the way to life, it is the way to finding your voice, but it is not going to be easy.

The Apostle Paul knew what his specific mission was: "…They saw that I had been entrusted with the task of preaching the gospel to the Gentiles, just as Peter had been to the Jews."[46]

John Wesley went through a significant personal spiritual journey, but it was not until George Whitefield invited him to leave the confines of church buildings and speak directly, in the open air to the poor, that he discovered his calling from God. The passage he spoke on would define the rest of his life's work of ministry to the poor of England, "The Spirit of the Lord is upon me, because He hath anointed me to preach the gospel to the poor."[47]

Hudson Taylor had already committed his whole life to God but he didn't know how or where and he wrote about the outcome of that wrestle: "Never shall I forget [he wrote long after] the feeling that came over me then. Words cannot describe it. I felt I was in the presence of God, entering into a covenant with the Almighty. I felt as though I wished to withdraw my promise but could not. Something seemed to say, 'Your prayer is answered; your conditions are accepted.' And from that time the conviction has never left me that I was called to China."[48]

General William Booth made it clear that from an early age he knew exactly what his life was to be about, "Sixty-Five years ago I chose the Salvation of me and the extension of the Kingdom of Jesus Christ as the supreme object for which I would live and labour … and that purpose is still, and will be to the end, the object which has shaped and mastered the thoughts, ambitions, and activities of my whole life."[49]

Mother Theresa spoke about a turning point in her life where, on a train journey she heard God say to her "Go to the poor. Leave the convent. Live with the poorest of the poor." From that point she was committed to a specific group of people.[50] To those who wanted to know how to make an impact like she had, Mother Theresa said: "Calcuttas are everywhere if only we have eyes to see. Find your Calcutta."[51]

5

Finding your Calcutta

Paul is clear that all of us, who profess a relationship with Jesus Christ, have been given a job to do: "All this is from God, who reconciled us to himself through Christ and gave us the ministry of reconciliation: that God was reconciling the world to himself in Christ, not counting people's sins against them. And he has committed to us the message of reconciliation."[32]   Each and every one of us is called to the remarkable task of helping the world find its right relationship with the maker of the universe. We are to do that through our actions (ministry) and the word of God (message). Each and every one of us has a job to do.

A very important theological understanding has gone missing from many churches, which is part of the reason we have fallen into the trap of the *Sacred-Secular Divide*. That is, we no longer really know what it means to *glorify God*. It is impossible to divide the world between sacred and secular once you catch a glimpse of what the writers of the Bible were trying to communicate through their many references to God's glory. *The glory of God* is a key to understanding what the Kingdom of God looks like in the context of a messy and sinful world. It helps to move the Kingdom of God from an abstract idea to a liveable reality.

The Christian church has always known that the glory of God is important. It is mentioned over one hundred times in the New Testament. The Westminster shorter catechism asserts that the chief end of man is to "glorify God and enjoy him forever". Biblical commentator, Matthew Henry wrote that God was pleased to "twist interests" with us, so that in seeking his glory, we are really seeking our own best interests.[53]

Unfortunately, the word *glory* conjures up pictures of either dazzling light or thunderous applause. In fact, one president of a Baptist seminary confided in me, that he had always seen the biblical references to God's Glory as being about God being self centred, wanting all of creation to be praising him. While this is a fairly normal perception, this is not at all what the writers of the bible understood glory to mean.

The fact that Jesus chooses the moment of his betrayal by Judas, and not the triumphal entry into Jerusalem to say "Now the Son of Man is glorified and God is glorified in him"[54] makes it clear that he didn't see glory in the way we normally use the word. Neither do other verses such as "all have sinned and fall short of the glory of God",[55] "Christ in you, the hope of glory"[56] and "This is to my Father's glory, that you bear much fruit",[57] fit with our normal use of the word glory.

So what is the Glory of God?

For the Hebrew people, the glory of God was at the heart of who they were. The Shekinah glory was the very presence of God that travelled with them and settled on the first temple. One of the defining interactions for them as a people, happened in Exodus 33 as Moses asks God "Now show me your glory."[58]

In Hebrew, the word 'glory' is *kabod* which means weight. When Moses asks to see God's glory he is, in effect, asking to see the full weight of who God is. God's response to Moses is that he would die if he was exposed to the full glory of God, but he could shelter in a cleft of a rock and as God passed before him, he could catch a glimpse of glory.

When God does pass in front of Moses, there is a bright light but it seems the glory of God is encapsulated in what God says about himself. What God is showing Moses is that his glory is not praise or applause, it his moral nature or how he chooses. As God passes in front of Moses, he proclaims "The LORD, the LORD, the compassionate and gracious God, slow to anger, abounding in love and faithfulness, maintaining love to thousands, and forgiving wickedness, rebellion and sin. Yet he does not leave the guilty unpunished; he punishes the children and their children for the sin of the parents to the third and fourth generation."[59] This is a densely packed couple of verses that many people, understandably, skip over, but in doing so they miss a critical key to understanding the Bible. In the two sentences of Exodus 34:6-7 we see both God's infinite love and at the same time, we see his unbending justice. As human beings we often see love and justice as mutually exclusive, but for God they are inseparable, and the foundation of his Kingdom.

The Glory of God, His justice and love is the pattern for redemption. The reason Jesus was able to say at the moment of his betrayal, "Now the Son of Man is glorified and God is glorified in him," is that the betrayal set in motion the events that led to the cosmic collision of the full weight of the justice of God with the full weight of the love of God, on the cross.

Charles Ryrie wrote that the glory of God is the "Character of God displayed."[60] God's glory is his moral nature, and our job is to bring the attributes of His nature to a world that is desperate for them. Richard R. Melick Jr. wrote "Those who understand Jesus' glory, by faith, are called to act according to what they have seen. They represent God's glory on earth by the values they hold as well as by their actions."[61] Our task is to bring God's justice and his love to the world, and as we find our particular way of working on that mission, we find, as Matthew Henry suggested, that we are actually seeking our own best interests.

The picture of love we see in the text is best captured by the words mercy, compassion and forgiveness. The Hebrew word for mercy most literally means, "seeing the world through another person's eyes". An old American

Indian saying goes, "You cannot judge a man until you have walked a mile in his moccasins". God enters our world and sees things through our eyes. In becoming human, Jesus was the embodiment of the mercy of God. *We are called to walk in this world with mercy, seeking first to understand and then be understood.*

In Latin, compassion means allowing yourself to suffer with someone. God is not a distant observer; he feels our pain and understands our confusion. *We are called to care, to allow ourselves to be affected by the sin and the mess of this world.*

When, on the cross, Jesus utters the words "It is finished",[62] he introduces the reality of a forgiveness that was the fulfilment of God's statement to Moses on Sinai. Forgiveness now means that the past can be over; the pain and hurt of the past are not to set the agenda for the future. *We are called to bring the healing balm of God's forgiveness to a world lost in a morass of evil and sin.*

God's justice comes from his righteousness. A friend of mine who is a Hebrew scholar helped me understand the implications of 'righteousness'. To be righteous is much more than 'acting right.' It means being in *right relationship* with God, yourself, other people and your environment. Right actions come from right relationship and justice defines that right relationship. Within the safety of just boundaries, it is possible to be free; as we step outside those boundaries, the consequences are real and lasting. Most of us would acknowledge that we carry scars from times we attempted to break life's boundaries, finding instead that it was we who were broken. In a proposal for the epic movie, *the Ten Commandments*, F.C. Nelson wrote to director Cecil B. DeMille, "You cannot break the Ten Commandments – they will break you."[63] *We are called to be agents of God's justice, restoring right relationship in a world of abuse and confusion.*

The Human spirit, that part of us created in the image of God, is most free, most alive within the framework of justice and love. Theologian Christopher Morgan writes "God's sharing of God's glory with us does not elevate us beyond our humanity or our nature as creatures but actually enables us to live in full humanness as image-bearers of God."[64] Human beings also instinctively recognise injustice and self interest, but sadly the normal response is to protect ourselves, which results in more injustice and self interest. The Glory of God lived out produces a virtuous cycle of justice and love. However as a person, family or nation walks away from justice and love, the outcome is dehumanising for everyone.

The wrong paths we have taken

Instead of the way of the justice and love, we Christians have broadly taken one of three other options. N.T. Wright, in the book *The Challenge of Jesus*, describes three groups of Jews at the time of Jesus who were doing the same thing. The first group, the *Quietists* escaped the world and retreated into a kind of super personal spirituality. The second group were the *Herodian* compromisers who lived their lives according to Roman rules, looking to stay safe and grow rich in the system of that world. The third group, the *Zealots*, wanted to fight power with power and worked to overthrow the Roman Empire and wrest control from Caesar.

There is a general trend in the West to an over-personalisation of Christianity. There are lots of Christians, often disaffected with their experience in congregations, who want to focus solely on how much Jesus loves them and avoid looking too closely at the world around them. As we accept the notion that faith is personal and has little implication for the issues of real world justice, we fall into the trap of the Quietists. This kind of Christianity expresses a strong focus on love and is suspicious of issues of justice. Its main agenda is set by personal feelings and it tends to lose sight of the world around it.

Some parts of the church fall into the trap of thinking that faith should lead you to what the world calls success. Church members become customers and evangelism becomes about sales and marketing. Church leaders drive expensive cars and prepare for the Sunday service in the same way a rock star prepares for a performance. This is nothing new; the Herodians were doing the same thing 2000 years ago. This kind of Christianity has its agenda set by the world and tends to focus on money and numbers and would see justice and love as a potential threat to the trappings of success.

The other trap that it is so easy for us to fall into is to think that the Kingdom of God can be brought to earth by force. If we can get control of the political structures, if we can get enough money or gain control of the media then we can change the world for Jesus. The Zealots tried grabbing power 2000 years ago. It didn't work then and it won't work now. This kind of Christianity often has an angry edge to it and tends to see people as enemies. The major focus is on justice, with love seen as too soft.

If the approaches of the Quietists, Herodians and Zealots were not what Jesus meant when he exhorted us to seek first the Kingdom, what did he mean? Somehow this Kingdom that was inaugurated with the birth of a baby in Bethlehem operates from a completely different set of rules.

Last year I travelled with my daughter to Poland where, after having an encouraging time with some very special believers who want to change their nation, we visited what is probably the site of the greatest evil this world has ever seen. I don't know how to describe the experience of Auschwitz. For the first time I could understand why people would want to deny the holocaust. As I looked at the mountain of gas canisters, the roll of material made from human hair and saw the site where experiments were carried out on children, a big part of me wanted to find a way not to face the reality of how disturbingly evil we can be to one another. It is hard for me to reconcile the idea that God's Kingdom is here, and yet something like this could happen.

A moment at Auschwitz will stay with me for the rest of my life. It was a moment that sharply focussed the difference between the Quietists, Herodians and Zealots and what the Kingdom of God actually is.

The way of the cross

We were taken down into a dark, cold and musty smelling basement that served as the cells of prisoners waiting for execution. Inside one of them was a big candle, which seemed incongruous in such a horrible place. Our tour guide told us about Maximilian Kolbe, a Polish priest who died as prisoner number 16770.

Fr. Kolbe had made a name for himself in the prison, quietly serving and comforting wherever he could. As a result he was singled out for special punishment and after one incident that nearly killed him, his response to his persecutors had such a profound effect on the German doctor that he later testified "I can say with certainty that during my four years in Auschwitz, I never saw such a sublime example of the love of God and one's neighbour."[65]

In July 1941, as punishment for the escape of a prisoner, ten men were randomly selected to be locked up without food and water until they died. One of them cried out that his wife and children needed him. Fr. Kolbe stepped forward and said, "I am a Catholic priest. Let me take his place. I am old. He has a wife and children."[66] Maximilian Kolbe was the last of the ten prisoners to die, his life ended by a lethal injection because he survived for so long without food or water.

In the moment, the commandant looked powerful, but it was the sacrifice of a brave Polish priest that continues to have impact today. He stood against injustice, not with force but as a powerful symbol of God's grace.

The way of the Kingdom is the way of the cross. We are called to bring redemption, to bring the glory of God, his justice and love, to the world in the place God has us, with the gifts and skills he has given us. We are called to go to the world in the same way Jesus went, with one hand reaching for the God of the universe and one hand grasping the pain of the injustice and self interest of a lost world.[67]

We hear the call as Jesus appears before his disciples in the upper room and says, "As the Father has sent me, I am sending you."[68] Five times in the Gospels Jesus exhorts his followers to be ready to take up their own crosses.[69]

Your mission will always be about glorifying God. It will be to make his nature, his justice and his love, manifest in the world. Charles Finney said,[70] "Every child of God is called to represent God, to be a teacher of God, to show forth to the world around him the character of God. Every saint is called of God to do this." [71]

John Stott wrote, "The followers of Jesus are to be different. Different from both the nominal church and the secular world, different from both the religious and the irreligious. The Sermon on the Mount is the most complete delineation anywhere in the New Testament of the Christian value-system, ethical standard, religious devotion, attitude to money, ambition, life-style and network of relationships - all of which are the total opposite of the non-Christian world. The Sermon presents life in the Kingdom of God, a fully human life indeed but lived out under the divine rule."[72]

We are called to live differently. We are called to bring our faith into the messy, dirty, confusing, tragic, hopeless, lost, scary places and reconcile those places to God. Our faith does not separate us from the world but places us at the very heart of the deepest pain. It is in this context that we find the purpose of our lives.

In seeking to live life from a value base of both justice and love, you will be creating the environment where both you, and those around you, actually experience a taste of the Kingdom of God. Through your life, there will be different specifics, but the general task will always be the same: to ask "where is injustice and self-interest?", and "how do I harmonize with the glory of God in order to respond here, with both justice and love?"

I hope you are feeling a little bit scared. You and I both know that neither of us is up to the job. In case we weren't absolutely sure, the Bible makes it clear that, "All have sinned and fall short of the glory of God."[73] This is one battle that you simply cannot fight on your own. The good news is you don't have to. Colossians 1:27 makes it abundantly clear that it is "Christ in you, the hope of glory."

6

Where is the Mission?

As we start to understand that our mission is about glorifying God, bringing his character to a world that desperately searches for hope, we need to explore the question of where and how that works.

We used to think of mission fields as being remote places like Africa and India; missionaries were "over there". We may not have realised it at the time, but that was a cop out. Now there is a greater understanding that we all have a mission field, wherever we are. In 1975, the founder of Youth with a Mission, Loren Cunningham, believed God showed him a different view of mission.[74] A day or so later he met Bill Bright, the founder of Campus Crusade and found that God had been saying the exact same thing to him. A few weeks later he discovered that author and founder of the L'Abri community, Francis Schaeffer, was talking about the same vision on national television. The realization was that mission was more than geographic. All three men believed God had shown them that the church needed to see the *different spheres* (taken from 2 Corinthians 10:13) of the world and to ensure that they each were being influenced by mission.

Loren outlined what he believed were the seven spheres in which the church needed to discover its ministry:

1.   The Home
2.   The Church
3.   Education
4.   Government and Politics
5.   The Media
6.   The Arts, Entertainment and Sports
7.   The Economy including Business and Science

This is an interesting and broad enough framework to create a space for most people to find their vocation in mission. I would also add healthcare and community services industries. These industries that were often started by Christians have become dominated by large N.G.O's and not-for-profit companies, and are a big enough sector in their own right to be an eighth sphere where Christians need to be bringing the redemptive love of Christ.

It may be that God is calling you to make a significant life altering decision because you know that the mission he has for you requires it, in the same way that my father did. More often than not, though, it will simply be a matter of seeing that God already has you in the place where he has called you to be an agent of his Kingdom. The circumstances of your life have brought you to this place and to this moment and your job is to accept the 'Calcutta' that is right in front of you. This does not mean you are called to a smaller, easier task than someone who senses their mission means major change, far from it. Your task is not business as usual, it is to see what the glory of God requires of you in that setting, name and accept the mission and begin.

In each of these areas we have had wonderful examples of Christians living their faith in ways that have been transformative; however lasting change seems to be brought not by individuals but by small groups of people. There is no doubt in my mind that the most effective way for you to work on your God given mission is within the context of a Kingdom Cell, a group of people who are similarly called to the frontier to which you are called.

One example of a Kingdom Cell is the "Inklings", a Kingdom Cell that included two of the most influential authors of the twentieth century. J.R.R. Tolkien and C.S. Lewis were both professors at Oxford University and good friends who formed the group and met together twice a week. The members believed in the power of the written word and the purpose of the group was for fellowship and for members to receive (often robust) criticism from others about their unfinished work.

Amongst the Inklings we see all the elements of the Kingdom Cell, but instead of changing a community they were wrestling with the world of literature. They were not working on a shared task, Tolkien alone wrote the Lord of the Rings, but as people who had a similar vocation, a similar mission, they were able to encourage, challenge and inspire one another. This kind of Kingdom Cell is most appropriate when a person's vocation is clearly an individual one, but where others have similar vocations. The creative arts, parenting and senior leadership in business are examples of vocations where this sort of Kingdom Cell might be the most helpful.

The Clapham Sect is another example of a Kingdom Cell that was transforming a different sphere: politics. Historian Stephen Tomkins describes them as "a network of friends and families in England, with William Wilberforce as its centre of gravity, who were powerfully bound together by their shared moral and spiritual values, by their religious mission and social activism, by their love for each other, and by marriage."[75] Historian, Dr. Marjorie Bloy, says of the Clapham Sect, "It is doubtful whether a single small congregation has in the history of Christendom exercised such a far-flung influence."[76]

This form of Kingdom Cell, with a significant shared external goal is the most effective way for Christians to work towards societal change, respond to need or effectively proclaim the gospel. Not every Kingdom Cell will have such profound and far reaching impact, but every Kingdom Cell will change the world as its members discover their vocation and pursue it. Mark Greene wrote, "Globally, 98% of Christians are neither envisioned nor equipped for mission in 95% of their waking lives. But just imagine if they were . . ."[77] Imagine what would happen, if there was an active Kingdom Cell in every one of Loren Cunningham's spheres, in every city on the earth!

7

Acting Symbolically

Once we have chosen our mission, we need to act. N.T. Wright, in the *Challenge of Jesus*, says "Your task is to find the symbolic ways of doing things differently, planting flags in hostile soil, setting up signposts that say there is a different way to be human."

When I first read Wright's statement, I wanted to protest. Symbolic action sounded like futile action. I wanted my action to be significant. I have often fallen into the trap of thinking like the Zealots, that I had to fix all the world's problems; that my job was done when everything was right with the world. Eventually the penny dropped. This world is broken and it is not my job to fix it, my job is to harmonise with God and work with my brothers and sisters in Christ to give a glimpse of a different, not so broken, way of doing life. Like Isaiah, we are called to be signs and symbols[78] in the face of a world that is based on self interest and greed.

Symbolic action is significant, not for what it is but for what it represents. Our actions have meaning, and for us to be agents of the Kingdom we need to make choices about behaviour that represents the values of the Kingdom. As we live like this, in a way that is so different to what is "normal" in a self interested and sinful world, people want to understand the meaning behind our actions. Wright suggests that was exactly how Jesus approached his mission. He would act symbolically, through healing, or speaking to someone others wouldn't, or eating with someone who was not politically correct, and then he would explain his actions through parables.

Major change happens when people start acting symbolically rather than fighting for control. William Wilberforce organised boycotts of children's sweets, had special jewellery made and organised a petition as part of his campaign to abolish slavery. One of Ghandi's most powerful actions was leading a march of hundreds of people to the sea in order to produce salt instead of buying it from the oppressive British regime. Martin Luther-King knew the power of symbolic action, and led several important marches but it was a brave African-American woman, Rosa Parks, whose symbolic action of not giving up a seat for a white passenger, became a symbol of the whole civil rights movement. One of the great gifts of the movie *Invictus* is the way it shows how clearly Nelson Mandela understood the importance of symbolic action, using sport to unite a nation. The Truth and Reconciliation Commission was an important symbolic statement by both Mandela and particularly Bishop Desmond Tutu, which enabled at least the potential for some of South Africa's wounds to begin to be healed.

A good friend of mine, Philemon, is working in Athens to bring hope in the midst of that nations desperate economic crisis. He and a group of young people who call themselves *Streetlights* are reaching for ways to act symbolically in the face of chaos. They don't have big budgets and most churches don't understand what they are trying to do, but there is a profound depth in their action and their communication which somehow cuts past the head and hits the heart. They are using modern multimedia to communicate, and although I often can't understand the words, the spirit of what they are doing is clear and moving.[79] One video in particular, of a young man acting symbolically in front of riot police, speaks very powerfully.[80]

I was interested to see Britain's most senior Roman Catholic, Cardinal Keith O'Brien, issue a call for Christians to start wearing crosses in a "simple and discreet way as a symbol of their beliefs."[81] He issued the call after a nurse and a flight attendant lost their jobs because they chose to wear the cross. In a politically charged environment, something as simple as wearing a cross can communicate more loudly than hundreds of words. I was interested in the way my youngest son responded to the news. He promptly purchased a cross and now both he and I wear them every day. It is a small action, but it is a symbolic action.

One of my friends has been through a horrific car accident which means that for the rest of his life he will battle daily with pain. Before the accident he was a well respected mime artist and one of the most touching things he did was a mime to a song about an Australian Jesus called "Red Prickle Beard". I will never forget the moment, a couple of years after the accident, when Steve believed God was inviting him to perform that mime again. As he was helped from his wheel-chair, he propped himself on a crutch with a look of shooting pain. The music began, and Steve forced his broken body to move in ways that it hadn't for two years. The choice to face the suffering to do what he believed God was asking of him spoke deeply to those who were there that night. At more than just one level, Steve was symbolically re-telling the story of Jesus.

One of the things I have both loved and hated about my ministry with Fusion has been the decision all senior Fusion workers make to live without a regular wage. This choice, based on our understanding of Jesus' promise in Matthew 6:33, means that Leeanne and I often experience real stress as we see bills come in without an obvious answer. It has also meant that I have found myself doing things like getting on an international flight with only twenty dollars in my pocket. I now realise that this choice is a symbolic choice. There is nothing wrong with having a wage, or even having lots of money, but by choosing to live as though God can be trusted to provide, we are symbolically standing against the values of a world that says your worth is valued by your bank account. It's amazing how many conversations this choice has prompted with people astonished that anyone could be so crazy as to try to live this way.

One of the most effective tools for ministry in community that I have seen is the *Open Crowd Festival*. It is effective because it is symbolic. For a moment, people are invited into a community of justice and love through the agency of a simple festival. When the festival works well, it is normal for people to come up to the organisers and want to join. They see something they cannot put into words, but know that it is "right".

In the little English village of Wheatley, churches have been putting on an Open Crowd festival for the last six years with a volunteer team of around 40 people and an average attendance of 700, almost 20% of the community. The Local United Reformed church minister captured the symbolic significance of the event when he said, "The fact that our churches are working together, side-by-side; people with deep faith and others of good will are experiencing the love and life of Christ, witnessing members of the body of Christ working as a united body. People from diverse backgrounds and worldviews sharing the same space and activities, creating an atmosphere of welcome and healthy community - these are all compelling signs of success to me. They bear witness to the presence and energy of God in our midst."

Most of us won't need to be acting symbolically to address issues that affect a whole nation, but that doesn't mean it will be any less powerful. Acting symbolically can happen in big and little ways. A mother who offers to help at her understaffed children's school is acting symbolically. A teenager who chooses to stand up for the victim of bullying is acting symbolically. A business that leaves its customers feeling valued is acting symbolically.

Symbolic action allows people to see and experience the Kingdom of God, and not just hear about it. People who see it will generally like what they are seeing. Acts 2 tells us that the early church enjoyed the favour of all the people.[82] The Kingdom of God is attractive. When people see the glory of God in action, at least some will find themselves attracted to what they see. Some people, however will sense that what they see threatens the very foundation on which they have built their life. The kingdom of God is threatening to those who are self centred, want power or love money. Not every time Christians are persecuted is it for their faith. There are many times we are persecuted because we are acting in a way that demonstrates our complete lack of awareness. Sometimes however, because the Kingdom of God represents a direct challenge to the values of the world, Christ followers will be persecuted simply for living from the Kingdom values of love and justice.

Being in the will of God, living out your vocation, doesn't mean you will have an easy time, in fact it almost guarantees the opposite. Romans 5:2-4 says "And we boast in the hope of the glory of God. Not only so, but we also glory in our sufferings, because we know that suffering produces perseverance; perseverance, character; and character, hope." It seems that there is actually a tie-up between the glory of God and our perseverance in suffering which ultimately produces hope. In John 20, before Jesus told the disciples they were sent in the same way he was, he showed them his hands and his side. He showed the scars of profound sacrifice and in effect said, "This was my turn, now it's your turn."

As I stood and stared at Nelson Mandela's Cell on Robben Island two years ago, I was hit by what it meant for him to be there. Mandela chose to give up his freedom in order to fight for freedom. I imagine there were times for him when everything in him was screaming to take an easier path. Mandela said *"There is no easy walk to freedom anywhere, and many of us will have to pass through the valley of the shadow of death again and again before we reach the mountaintop of our desires."*[83]

8

Entering the Dialogue

As you set out on your particular mission, it can be tempting to look for shortcuts and want to take a program or idea that someone else invented in another time or place and use it in your context. The *E-myth* by Michael Gerber and franchises like McDonalds made the idea of *turnkey* businesses popular. The idea behind a turnkey business is that someone with no prior knowledge or experience should be able to walk in, read the manual, and successfully operate the business. While a simple, reproducible model works well for hamburgers, it doesn't work for the Kingdom of God. One way the Kingdom Cell differs from the biological cell is that biological separation produces two identical Cells, whereas healthy Kingdom Cells will always take on a different shape and form depending on their context.

Part of the reason I refer to so many different figures from church history in this book is that they each had to find a way to bring the life of the Kingdom of God into their own unique context. Basil was living in a very different world to Wilberforce, and Wilberforce accepted a very different mission to Wesley. Each of them referred to the word of God, and to the heroes of the past, but each one also had to find a new response to new questions. This is what Jesus is getting at when he says "Therefore every teacher of the law who has become a disciple in the kingdom of heaven is like the owner of a house who brings out of his storeroom new treasures as well as old." To seek first the Kingdom is to embark on a journey that will require you to treasure and learn from those who have gone before you, yet also to be continually ready with a new response to a new set of questions: to create new treasures for the Kingdom.

The time we are in, lends itself to the church rediscovering this more biblical, dialogical approach to mission. In the book, *Leadership Next*, Eddie Gibbs says "The new realities of post modernity mean that the church must be fluid, flexible and capable of adjusting to diversity. It can expand as a movement only to the extent that it is made up of small reproducible units. However, the reproduction of these units must happen, not through mass production or mere replication, but through a process of generation that, in accordance with particular mission challenges and cultural contexts, encourages great variety."[84]

As I have observed the Fusion movement, with which I am most familiar, there has been a clear expansion of focus from simple gospel preaching in the early 1960s to a more integrated approach to mission focused on need. Each Fusion centre around the world starts with two essential ingredients: prayer and research. Prayer means we are looking at a community with God and asking for his wisdom. In this context research means moving beyond our own pre-conceptions about what the needs of the community might be, to actually allowing God to show us the things that matter to him. This is what Paul was doing as he walked around Athens and what Nehemiah did as he inspected the wall. This approach means that in some communities Fusion is providing accommodation for homeless young people, in others, support for single mothers and in others, mental health services. In each community though, the Fusion team is working towards a vision of the same Kingdom. Being continually on the front edges of community need and searching for real and effective ways to respond rather than following the format of a program, means that Fusion is continually learning.

This approach to Kingdom mission would be called "dialogical" by author and educator, Paulo Friere. In his book, *Pedagogy of the Oppressed*, Friere highlighted two different approaches to education. The first approach he called banking education[85] where teachers focused on depositing the right words and ideas into student's brains so they could be regurgitated when it came to exam time. This model puts the teacher above the student as the expert, and usually means the teacher is communicating insights they have learned from somebody else in the same way. The second approach he called dialogical education where teachers focus the students on the questions presented by life, and both the teachers and students sit together under the reality they are facing, and learn together. This model of education puts the teacher on the same level as the student as a fellow traveller. Whenever the Christian church is at its best, it is truly dialogical in its approach to living faith, and is constantly learning and changing.

Bringing the Kingdom of God to a community

Marg Fletcher is a hero of mine. Marg has been a resident of the tiny Australian country town of Coleambally (or Coly as the locals call it) for longer than I have been alive. She loves the town with a love that is infectious. She is known by all the local teenagers, and they will often stop her in the street just for a chat. Marg is continually working to help the couple of local churches love the community like she does.

A number of years ago I travelled to Coleambally to do some training for the local team and Marg proudly showed me the brand new one bedroom flat she had built out the back of her house. She knew that Coly needed a youthworker and she built the flat for the person that she knew God would provide. I didn't have the heart to tell her that the chances of a trained youth worker coming to the tiny town were slim, particularly as there was no hope of any kind of wage. While Marg waited she undertook Youth work training herself. In her 70s she was the oldest in the classroom by at least three decades but undeterred she gathered a little team around her and they went to work.

As I write this, Coly has a youth worker, a youth cafe and some of the most loved young people in New South Wales. Through her humble commitment to her town, Marg has changed the lives of many young people over the past decades, and has helped the local churches find a deep connection with the local community. In 2011 Marg was recognised as the Coleambally's "Citizen of the Year".

Francis Tsimese is another hero of mine. I first met Francis when he travelled from Ghana to Australia for training in youth and community work. He travelled with two others from the Ghana Baptist church, and about four months into his stay, his two travelling companions disappeared into suburban Melbourne, opting for the life of an illegal immigrant rather than return home.

Francis was desperately homesick and in severe culture shock. He says it was a trip to Uluru, the massive red monolith in the heart of Australia that helped him find his bearings. As he saw the young people engaging with Aboriginal culture and discovering faith for themselves, somehow he discovered his own purpose: he was committed to Ghana.

He soaked up the training and after 18 months, headed back to a small city in Northern Ghana called Yendi. He believed the principles he had seen at work in Australia, if adapted to Ghanaian culture, could help change that nation. Yendi is primarily a Muslim community where bouts of tribal violence can be a real issue. The Christian churches had not really worked together very well, and just finding water to drink can be a serious issue during summer. Francis believed God had asked him to commit to Yendi. A team formed around him and they established Yendi's first community centre. He created a volleyball court on the dirt ground and marked out a soccer pitch. The community centre is now a hive of activity, with fifty or sixty kids turning up for 'Sports for Hope' each afternoon. He has encouraged the churches to work together, particularly at Christmas and Easter. He is trying to work with the Ghanaian government to gain permission for Yendi to have its own radio station, because there currently is no way to communicate with the whole region. He built connections with the Muslim community, and after recently being away for three months, the community threw a big celebration on his return. Yendi is different because Francis Tsimese and his team committed to a community.

Marg and Francis are both part of a special kind of Kingdom Cell, one committed to a whole community. They both created a framework that enabled lots of different people, including churches, to engage with the community in lots of different ways. Time and time again I have seen the significant impact of a small group of friends who commit like this, to working for the Kingdom of God in a suburb, town or village. A friend and senior Anglican minister spelled out for me how commitment to a geographical community lies at the heart of their tradition. As a rector accepts his pastoral appointment, he is reminded that his flock is not just those who turn up to church on Sunday, but all those who live within the parish. He or she accepts the burden of responsibility for the "cure of souls" in a whole community.

While not everyone is called to this kind of commitment to a whole community, I believe that there is something particularly important about this particular kind of Kingdom Cell in the re-igniting of the radical movement that the body of Christ truly is.

A dream I have is that we will one day see at least one Kingdom Cell committed to every village, suburb and town in the world. At least one group of friends, who love Jesus and have committed themselves to the fight for the Kingdom of God in that place, would begin a chain reaction to free others to find their vocation in all kinds of ways. The world would change.

Power vs. Authority

Both Marg and Francis have gained significant authority in their communities. As you follow the path to which God calls you, you too will find that your personal authority will grow as you pursue a life marked by love and justice. Tremper Longman III wrote, "Thanks to the work of God, God's people are "heavy" with significance... They have substance and reputation ("you shall be called by a new name," Is 62:2). God's blessing will also bring them substance. Their glory primarily serves a missionary purpose, as the nations will see this glory and be attracted to it."[86] I have seen the truth of what Longman wrote over and over again. Authority though, is a different thing to power.

The disciples believed that the Messiah would take power from the Romans and re-establish the Jewish nation. At one point, two of the disciples had their mother ask Jesus if they could have special privileges and extra power in his Kingdom. Jesus used the moment to illustrate the difference between how the world works and how his kingdom works. He said, "You know that the rulers of the Gentiles lord it over them, and their high officials exercise authority over them. Not so with you. Instead, whoever wants to become great among you must be your servant, and whoever wants to be first must be your slave — just as the Son of Man did not come to be served, but to serve, and to give his life as a ransom for many."[87] Jesus tries to make it clear that the Kingdom of God is not about power.

Power, according to respected German sociologist, Max Weber,[88] is to have the coercive force to make others yield to your wishes, even against their will. In a normal organisational structure, the person at the top of the pyramid has the power to determine the shape and form of a person's employment, their ability to terminate a person's employment and their ability to determine how much money their employees receive. All of these things represent a degree power.

Eugene Peterson is very clear about the implications of power for the Kingdom of God: "The moment the community exercises power apart from the story of Jesus, tries to manipulate people or events in ways that short circuit personal relationships and intimacies, we can be sure it is not the power of the Holy Spirit; it is the devil's work."[89]

Weber distinguished between authority and power. He said that authority is given to someone by people who choose to follow them.[90] Authority can never be taken, only given. As I have already said, the word Glory means weight in Hebrew. Whenever God's people have been at their best, they have been people who sought to glorify God. They are agents of both love and justice, and as a result gain moral authority.

One person who exemplifies the authority that comes from seeking justice and love is Mother Theresa. In 1994, when asked to address the National Prayer Breakfast, Mother Theresa rose from the table of honour to deliver a stinging attack on the position taken by the President of the United States and his wife on abortion.[91] Bill and Hilary Clinton could only sit and listen as they were chastised, "Any country that accepts abortion is not teaching the people to love, but to use any violence to get what they want. That is why the greatest destroyer of love and peace is abortion." The man, who is supposed to be the most powerful person in the world, was scolded like a naughty boy by a diminutive nun from Calcutta. The person who harmonises with God's glory, finds themselves gaining moral authority that comes no other way.

Christian author and sociologist, Tony Campolo relates his experience of leading a seminar on the difference between power and authority, during which a political exile from the Philippines, Benigno Aquino, was in the audience. Aquino had been a senator and opposition leader against the dictatorial presidency of Ferdinand Marcos and had been gaoled by Marcos. Allowed to travel to the U.S. for medical treatment, he decided to go home following the treatment, knowing he was powerless in the face of the Marcos political and military machine. After Campolo's lecture, Aquino told him, "You have given me hope. I know that when I return to my homeland, I will be powerless, but you have helped me to see that I still can have authority. What I say is right, and the people know it, what I believe to be true. I love my people and I am willing to die for them, and I now believe that if I sacrifice my personal safety I will have great influence in the Philippines, even though I will have no power at all." [92]

In an interview aboard the plane that was carrying him home, Benigno told reporters, "I suppose there's a physical danger because you know assassination's part of public service. My feeling is we all have to die sometime and if it's my fate to die by an assassin's bullet, so be it."[93]

Even before he stepped off the plane, Benigno Aquino was shot by an assassin wearing a military uniform. His death galvanised the people of the Philippines, Marcos had power, but he lost authority. Three years later Benigno's wife Corazon was elected President of the Philippines, ending Marcos' despotic regime. Benigno Aquino's love for his people and willingness to lay down his life for their sake brought about a revolution. Aquino had learned that authority and power were two very different things.

What is your mission?

So it comes down to a simple question: What is your mission?

Satan has an investment in you not having one. He is happy for you to go along to church on Sundays, listen to worship music, read your Bible and even pray, but if you start to understand that God is inviting your partnership in establishing his Kingdom on earth as it is in heaven, Satan won't like it. To commit to a mission requires a choice. You might be a mum, a student, an artist or a businessperson. Do you know what your mission is in your context? You might be sensing a call to change a community. Are you ready to make a choice to do it? Are you ready to find friends who can stand with you in the mission God has called you to?

Once you let Jesus be King of your life and not just King of your belief system, you have already moved into mission, whether you realise it or not. Sometimes, some parts of your mission will be crystal clear, as the abolition of slavery was for Wilberforce, or as helping our kids grow up to be the men and women God created them to be, is for Leeanne and I. Other parts of your vocation might become clearer over time like this whole idea of Kingdom Cells has been for me. This book has come from my personal wrestle with what it is God is asking of me, and the Kingdom Cell has been my best attempt at explaining it to myself and others. The mission I am committed to is seeing Kingdom Cells within reach of every person in the world and in the institutions and networks that shape our lives, like business, media and government. I have known the truth of the Kingdom Cell intuitively for most of my life but it is only in the last few years that I have found a form of words for what has been in my heart.

I meet many people who, like me who intuitively know a general direction that God is inviting them to, but it is in living with the frustration of not fully being able to describe it that it actually starts to take shape. Commitment to a mission requires commitment even before you can clearly articulate what the mission is. The very act of setting sail is important in the process of discovery. If you wait in the harbour until you have a completely planned trip, you will never leave. So, however clear or unclear you believe your vocation is, get started. If you don't know where to start, your neighbourhood is always a safe bet. Jesus' injunction to love our neighbours was meant as more than a general suggestion. Don't wait to *feel*, start to *do*. There are plenty of people and organisations who will be willing to give you a hand to get started. [94]

If you have a job, start to see it for what it is: a ministry. You have the remarkable task of bringing the glory of God into the workplace. Dream about what is possible. As you begin to act, your mission will become clearer and clearer.

Some of the vocations that can have the deepest personal impact on another person are also the vocations that our society overlooks, like being a mother or being a nurse. One evening the wife of author and sociologist Tony Campolo was asked what she did by someone who obviously thought they were her superior. Campolo recalls his wife's response with pride, "I am socializing two homo sapiens into the dominant values of the Judeo-Christian tradition in order that they might be the instruments for the transformation of the social order into the kind of teleologically prescribed utopia inherent in the eschaton!"[95] We need more mothers like Peggy Campolo, who can proudly stand up and claim the truth of their calling to that vocation.

No matter what mission you accept as yours, it will mean moving beyond safety, into a real world of hurting people. One of the dangers for anyone who wants to take mission seriously is that, simply to survive, we are tempted to develop a distance between ourselves and those we are called to serve. Whether it be salesmen, social workers, pastors or even parents, it can be easier to adopt a persona and keep relationships to a very superficial level. The thing is, people can tell.

In Romans 9:1-4 the Apostle Paul admitted to carrying a continual low-lying grief for his people: "I speak the truth in Christ—I am not lying, my conscience confirms it in the Holy Spirit—I have great sorrow and unceasing anguish in my heart. For I could wish that I myself were cursed and cut off from Christ for the sake of my brothers, those of my own race, the people of Israel."

At another point when he was in Athens we see how Paul lets himself be affected by the city: "While Paul was waiting for them in Athens, he was greatly distressed to see that the city was full of idols."[96] The shortest verse in the Bible is "Jesus wept."[97] Jesus let himself be affected as he saw the grief of his close friends. Jesus cared, Paul cared, and if we are to truly glorify God, we too, need to do the risky thing of making ourselves vulnerable enough to actually care.

If your vocation is as an artist, helping people see the world and themselves in a new way, you will need to care.

If your vocation is to love and prepare your children to discover their vocation in the world, you will need to care.

If your vocation is to serve on a factory floor where people are being treated as extra pieces of machinery, you will need to care.

If your vocation is to lead a business to operate from the values of the Kingdom and help both staff and customers become more the people they were created to be, you will need to care.

The most important thing is to make a choice and start. You don't need to have all the answers and as you begin there is no real way of knowing where you will end. The one thing you can be sure of though, is that God is with you.

If a small group of people can put their love for Jesus first, and then in response to that love open themselves to a mission that reflects the concerns of the Kingdom of God, then the world can indeed change.

9

The Third Radical Decision: Fellowship

Basil was brilliant. He was the smartest in his class and ran rings around most of his university professors. Unfortunately, he knew he was smart and tended to treat others with contempt. That was until the day his big sister had had enough of his attitude and told him off. Somehow her words got through his guard and triggered a crisis in his confidence. He sought to understand what was happening to him and found a copy of the Bible. A brilliant Greek scholar, the truth he was reading spoke to the core of who he was as a human being.

He began to let go of his trust in his own capacity and began the lifelong wrestle of putting his trust in Jesus. Before long he knew he needed help, not from scholars but from people who were truly living out their faith. Basil went on a tour, visiting some of the most radical Christians he could find, but ultimately he came home both challenged and a little bit disappointed. He had met people who were very committed but there was something missing. He wanted to give Jesus everything, so he found a place to be by himself and attempted to live each day fully committed to Christ. He had thought that somehow he could escape sin if he was on his own, but like most of us, he discovered that no matter where we go we take our biggest problem with us, and that is <u>us</u>.

We have the letter he wrote out of desperation to his close friend Gregory (St. Gregory the Theologian) asking him to come and join him because he needed both the company and the accountability. Basil wrote "I carry my own troubles with me, and so everywhere I am in the midst of similar discomforts. So in the end I have not got much good out of my solitude."[98]

His letter to Gregory goes on to outline a dream for a different way of living which became the basis for the Basilian monastic movement and made 'Basil the Great' one of the most important figures in church history. He and Gregory, along with his brother (also Gregory), formed the nucleus of a fellowship that would help transform Europe. Together they fought for the truth of the Trinity and helped hammer out one of the foundational documents of the Christian church, the Nicene Creed.

My friend Bruce Dutton explored some of Basil's story and wrote about it for an Australian Christian magazine. He points out that Basil's monks "were not just to care for the welfare of their own souls. They were also to care for and encourage one another in their discipleship."[99] He also said, "They were to "help carry one another's burdens" (Galatians 6:2); to "be eager to show respect for one another" (Romans 12:10); to be "tolerant with one another" (Ephesians 4:2); to be "kind and tender hearted to one another, forgiving one another" (Ephesians 4:32); "to provoke one another to love and good works" (Hebrews 10:24); to "submit to one another" (Ephesians 5:21) and to confess their faults to one another, and to pray for one another"(James 5:16)."[100] Most of Basil's longer and shorter rules came directly from the Bible.

A few years after setting up the religious order, Basil hit one more identity crisis, as he realized his team had become too insular and too safe. He led his brothers out of the cloister to serve the poor and needy in the local community. Basil became the local bishop, using the local church as a kind of community centre for the whole region. Something remarkable happened: the whole community was transformed.

Basil's discovery of a personal relationship with Jesus, a choice to find fellowship and then his choice to take on the mission of the poor in the community had a significant impact. The choices he made in 300 A.D. not only transformed his local community, but the impact of Basil's band of brothers spread around the world. In 2007, Pope Benedict said, "... St. Basil created a special kind of monasticism, not closed off from the local Church, but open to it. His monks were part of the local Church, *they were its animating nucleus*[101]. Preceding others of the faithful in following Christ and not merely in having faith, they showed firm devotion to him -- love for him -- above all in works of charity. These monks, who established schools and hospitals, were at the service of the poor and showed Christian life in its fullness."[102] I have already discussed the primary importance of a real relationship with Christ, and then resulting from that, the choice to accept a mission. What is also clear is that Basil, Wesley, the Clapham Sect, the Inklings, the Disciples and almost any other moment in history where the church has been at its best, all had something in common: they all took the risky step of real fellowship.

In his paper, *The church as the servant of the New Europe*, Duncan B. Forrester argues that, "The most significant fruit of the Pauline project was probably the establishment gradually throughout Europe of communities of faith which nurtured and explored the idea of fellowship and opened up a range of new possibilities in a situation of social decadence. Sheldon Wolin argues that it was these marginalised little Christian communities, struggling to be fellowships of love without compromises with power, which revitalized political thought by demonstrating that a better structuring of human relationships was possible, that it 'worked'."[103]

The Bible makes it clear how fundamentally important real fellowship is for followers of Jesus. Romans 12:10 challenges us to "Be devoted to one another in love. Honour one another above yourselves." 1 Peter 1:22 exhorts us to "love one another deeply, from the heart." Jesus leaves no room for mistake when he says, "A new command I give you: Love one another. As I have loved you, so you must love one another. By this everyone will know that you are my disciples, if you love one another."[104]

How are we going at being a fellowship of love?

The Western world is organized around the principle of the primacy of the individual, and so too is much of the Western church. A case could be put that we use the language of fellowship and community but generally stay safely distant from each other. One of the most powerful questions I ask when speaking to Christians is, "How many people would you say really know what life is like for you?"[105] Inevitably a hush comes over the room as people come face to face with their isolation. Often I will get those who would think more than 10 people know what life is like for them to raise their hand. In a room of 100 people, maybe one or two people might tentatively raise a hand. I will reduce the number to 5 people, and maybe another 3 or 4 people might put up their hand, but by far the majority of people indicate that they have no-one in that category. Why is it like this?

We know fellowship is important, and yet most of us live our lives in isolation from those closest to us. One of the sad things about life is that we all start, as children, open, free and trusting and then gradually as pain piles on hurt, piles on misunderstanding, we learn it is safer to be less free, less open and less trusting. The pain of our experiences of relationships as we grow, gradually wraps the butterfly back into the cocoon. We learn how to play the game, to look ok even when inside we are desperate for someone, anyone, to know us.

Howard Snyder, in his book, *New Wineskins*, says "The church today is suffering a fellowship crisis. It is simply not experiencing nor demonstrating that "fellowship of the Holy Spirit" (2 Corinthians 13:14) that marked the

New Testament church. In a world of big, impersonal institutions, the church often looks like just another big, impersonal institution. The church is highly organised just at the time when her members are caring less about organisation and more about community."[106]

If we truly want to see the Kingdom of God come on earth as it is in heaven, then we need to find a way to connect with each other.

Real fellowship, that encourages, helps me see myself and that helps me understand what life is like for others, is the other key element in our journey towards maturity.

How do we find fellowship?

The best image of fellowship I have come across is Proverbs 27:17: "As iron sharpens iron, so one man sharpens another." I get the picture that we start out like big uneven lumps of raw metal, and then gradually as we bang up against one another, the uneven bits fly off and we are honed into a sharp blade that becomes increasingly effective at sharpening others.

The truth that this Proverb clearly communicates is that in order to have fellowship you need to be iron; anything softer will do nothing at all. You are on a journey to be you. There is a kind of fellowship you can have with people who never disagree. It can appear on the surface to be quite pleasant and conversations can be broad and varied, but ultimately nobody will ever really meet anyone else. To have real fellowship takes a real choice; the choice to be real and to allow others to be real, to allow the iron to meet iron. It was this kind of fellowship that saved my marriage.

I married Leeanne when I was 22. At the time I thought I was fairly mature but as I look back now I feel a bit embarrassed at how self centred I was. I remember the profound sense of shock as I gradually realised just how different we were. I started to build a mental list of all the ways Leeanne was getting it wrong. We found it progressively harder and harder to talk. Finally I shared my concerns with a close friend, Dave, who was almost ten years older than me and someone who I was learning to trust. His response was disturbing. He laughed. "Let me get this straight," he said "Your marriage is in trouble and its <u>all</u> Leeanne's fault?" Dave didn't have to say anything else, the penny dropped with a thud. For the first time (I told you that I wasn't particularly aware at the time) I started to realise that a marriage takes two people. I am grateful that Dave didn't just tell me what I wanted to hear, but metaphorically held a mirror up so that I could catch a glimpse of just how self centred I was being. This kind of real fellowship is most likely to happen in a relationship where it is safe to disagree. This requires commitment from both sides.

The Greek word *perichoresis* is a picture of what real fellowship is all about. The word doesn't come from the Bible, but from the early church fathers who were looking to describe the relationship of the Trinity. Baxter Kruger, one of the thinkers at the forefront of the discussion of Trinitarian theology, describes perichoresis as "mutual indwelling without loss of identity". The picture is captured in Jesus' words, "Believe me when I say that I am in the Father and the Father is in me." The Father was 'in' Jesus, and Jesus was 'in' the Father and still they were both clearly individuals. This is the picture we have of the Holy Trinity: three individuals who are 'in' each other but still maintain their individuality.

Perichoresis would simply be an intellectual exercise, if not for the fact that we are created in the image of God, a God who exists in perfect community, and therefore we hunger for Trinitarian relationships. When I introduced the Glory of God, I pointed out that two aspects of God's character are his absolute justice and his absolute love; it is these two things together that create the framework for the Trinitarian fellowship that we long for. It is God's love, and particularly his mercy that means that all three members of the Trinity are 'in' each other. It is God's justice, which means that they do not lose their identity in their fellowship.

In healthy fellowship, I allow another person to enter my heart. I "Rejoice with those who rejoice; mourn with those who mourn."[107] I allow myself to be deeply affected by the other. In this though, I don't lose my identity. I don't become them. In healthy community I become more myself as I open myself to others.

Bands of brothers (and sisters)

I love the title of the television mini-series *Band of Brothers*. I think part of the success of that series was that we all long for that kind of fellowship: the small group of friends who have your back while together you do the impossible. As I look at church history it has been the bands of brothers (and sisters), the Kingdom Cells, that changed the world.

Part of what distinguishes a Kingdom Cell from a church small group or a business fellowship group is a shared mission. It is this shared mission that is also a key to their fellowship. Allan Hirsch quotes author Victor Turner in his book *The Forgotten Ways* to explain this deeper kind of connection. He says "*Communitas* in (Turner's) view *happens* in situations where individuals are driven to find each other through a common experience of ordeal, humbling, transition, and marginalization. It involves intense feelings of social togetherness and belonging brought about by having to rely on each other in order to survive."[108] Whenever I have talked to war veterans, they tell me that the relationship you build with those you have served with cannot be put into words. There is a deep and real commitment that comes from being shoulder to shoulder in the face of adversity.

Hirsch says "Communitas can be at work in less hazardous situations, like sports teams, where a group of otherwise individualistic people band together to achieve a common task. They become a team around a common challenge."[109] The high points of my ministry have been the times when I have been part of a team standing shoulder to shoulder in the face of a difficult challenge. Sometimes this has been a particular program, such as a massive stadium event or a secondary school student leadership program that we had to make up as we went. Twice it has been with teams that worked together for several years.

The first time I learned the significance of *communitas* was when I found myself in over my head. I had been working with Fusion for three years and was newly married. I had lost three whole teams of people who had come, got inspired, and left, usually as a result of my lack of awareness. My naive optimism from my days in Fusion's Bible College had been well and truly knocked out of me.

As I was coping with my personal identity crisis, an opportunity arose for Fusion to take on the responsibility for a municipal council youth service. The council understood fully that we were a Christian organisation, and the local churches were all quite pleased with the prospect. Our job was to establish a Youth Cafe, run youth work in secondary schools and advise council on Youth policy. This was great, and Fusion over the years had lots of resources and experience, but I didn't. I also didn't have a lot of self confidence after what felt like three years of failure.

Into this setting came a 17 year old who had just completed Fusion's training and was coming to work with me as a student on placement. Jev, as she preferred to be known, had soaked in Fusion's certificate course like a sponge, and wasn't jaded from three years of failure. She would ask obvious questions like "shouldn't we pray before opening the cafe?" and all the kids knew she loved them. Gradually things started to change. My mate Dave drove down from Poatina every week to help with training, and as we connected with local churches and started a weekly prayer breakfast, the team started to grow. A down to earth carpenter who installed wood heaters, Chris, did the training we ran and offered to come and run monthly day-trips for the young people. A retired businessman mentored me with the finances and found a very special woman, Carol, to manage the office (which was in severe need of managing!). Edwina, joined the team from Sydney with some natural management skill, and an energetic young woman, Lisa, took on responsibility for our schools work. People from local churches started to join the team and lots of young people were having their lives changed. None of us had much experience but within 18 months we were working with 25% of the teenagers in the area. By the time that another youth worker, Kathy, joined us, the ministry was growing rapidly. We enjoyed each other's company, but more than that, we depended on each other almost as much as we depended on Jesus.

The other time I have experienced *communitas* over a longer period of time was with the team in Victoria. As I have already shared with you, I was weary and probably burned out, and I was going into a place where every leader had left over the course of the previous twelve months. The conference where it was announced that my predecessor was leaving and I was coming in is a vivid and emotional memory. Fusion was preparing to run a mission training program, connected with the Commonwealth Games in Melbourne 12 months after I arrived. Students were coming from all over the world to learn how to do mission, and the centres where they were meant to be learning were all in serious trouble.

I clearly recall speaking with Steve, an accountant who had been around the edges of Fusion for a number of years and was someone I trusted, and saying, "Mate, I need your help." I met with three ladies who had all been working with Fusion in Victoria and as I heard their hearts, I invited each of them to step into leadership. I remember looking around the table at our first executive meeting at our leadership team, none of whom had been in leadership like this before and wondering if there was any hope at all that we would succeed. We started to come together across the state each Monday to pray, share and open the Word of God together and gradually we became a team.

We all knew that we needed each other and we needed God. He didn't let us down. The first 18 months were crazy, but the team grew remarkably. We had 45 students from nine countries join us for two months, and we started two new outreach centres. At one point we did the numbers and between our six centres in Victoria, we were working directly with over 1,800 young people a week, between 20 and 30 young people were coming to faith every month, and every 12 months we were accommodating over 300 homeless teenagers. We enjoyed each other's company, and there was a very special sense of being "in it together" for much of the time.

I have also seen the link between having a mission and the ability to actually experience fellowship where I live in Poatina, Tasmania. Poatina is not a normal town. We established it to be a model of the old Indian proverb, 'It takes a village to raise a child', and over the last 16 years several hundred young people (and some older people) have been helped to deal with critical issues in their lives after spending time there. We have a rule of thumb that for every 100 village residents, we can care for 10 who need help (five with significant needs and five with less significant needs). There are about 120 permanent residents and most of them have become multi-skilled, regularly volunteering in the local shop, service station or motel, all of which are run completely by volunteers.

Whenever I speak about Poatina I can make it sound fantastic. The reality though is that welcoming people with challenges into your life is very difficult, and just because you call a bunch of people a community doesn't mean they are. I think we come and go from community in this village, and a large part of that is dependent on whether people are committed to a shared mission or committed to themselves. I must confess that as an individual I come and go from both polarities and as a result so does my experience of community. In Poatina it is clear that real fellowship comes as a by-product of serving together. Those who are least willing to serve are those who least experience community. The moments where we are 'in it together' though, are those I look back on as some of the richest experiences in my life.

Communitas is much more than an academic concept. There is simply something special that happens when a small group of people love Jesus and commit themselves to a goal that none of them can do on their own. The relationship that builds between them becomes deep and rich and remains as a point of reference for the rest of their lives.

10

The Few

Throughout the history of the church, Kingdom Cells have been small groups. They have however, often had significant networks of friends and acquaintances.

One of the things I found helpful in visualising the Kingdom Cell in the diagram was realising that relationships happened at least at three levels. At the core there is the small group, the band of friends, where fellowship is deepest and most real because of their shared commitment both to Christ and a shared mission. This is where Basil and the two Gregorys stood shoulder to shoulder, where C.S. Lewis and Tolkien had their long walks, where Paul and Barnabas faced the music together.

When I see a basketball team who have played together for a while on court, it is obvious. So often one player will throw the ball not to where his team-mate is, but where he will be by the time the ball arrives. They instinctively know each other's strengths and weaknesses and seemingly effortlessly toss the ball to each other. This is the image that comes to mind when I reflect on my experiences of being in the core of a Kingdom Cell in Southern

Tasmania then in Victoria. In both places we worked very hard, but there was something about being in it together, knowing that someone has your back, that just can't be captured in words.

This core of a Kingdom Cell is always a small group that is usually between three and five and almost never more than twelve. Robin Dunbar, a Professor of Anthropology at the University of Oxford, hypothesizes that the maximum number of intimate relationships people have is between five and seven. He believes that the maximum number of less intimate friends you can have is 150.[110] If the number at the core grows too big, the group is faced with the dilemma of either splitting into smaller groups or moving to a less personal organisational structure and sacrificing the level of fellowship that is so crucial.

The Kingdom Cell is more than just the core group though. The diagram shows a group of people inside the Cell but not in the centre. Not everyone will be ready to commit to your mission at the same level you are, but that doesn't mean they are not a vital part of the team. William Pitt was not at the core of the Clapham Sect and he was suspicious of his friend, William Wilberforce's discovery of faith, however he was committed to both his friend and to the abolition of slavery. For Pitt, however, abolition was not his main agenda, leading the country was. It is doubtful Wilberforce would have succeeded without Pitt, but for Pitt the mission of the Clapham Sect was a secondary one. In the same way, all those who collected petitions and acted locally were not at the core of the Clapham Sect, but Wilberforce and his friends would not have got very far without them.

As I will discuss in the next two chapters, one of the dangers for a Kingdom Cell is that those at the core enjoy each other's company too much and become exclusive. The moment this happens they cease to be a Kingdom Cell and become a club.

The other danger is that a group of people who are primarily committed to other things will come together for a mission and be surprised when it doesn't last. Without the core of people who are committed to Christ, committed to the mission and committed to each other, a Kingdom Cell is more of a Kingdom doughnut: it tastes good but it has a hole in the middle and there is not a lot of lasting value.

Fellowship is vital in order to know the will of God

Part of the reason real fellowship is so important is that our ability to separate the chaos of our souls from the quiet truth of the Holy Spirit is extremely limited, and in addition to that, our view of the world is always limited and subjective. We need honest fellowship in order to live in truth. I don't think it is an accident that 1 John 1:7 seems to tie being able to 'walk in the light' with having fellowship: "But if we walk in the light, as he is in the light, we have fellowship with one another, and the blood of Jesus, his Son, purifies us from all sin."

Dietrich Bonhoeffer wrote: "Christians need other Christians who speak God's word to them. They need them again and again when they become uncertain and disheartened because, living by their own resources, they cannot help themselves without cheating themselves out of the truth."[iii]

Jesus makes the importance of fellowship in knowing God's will clear in Matthew 18:19, but unfortunately the meaning of the text often gets lost in translation. He says, "Again, I tell you that if two of you on earth agree about anything you ask for, it will be done for you by my Father in heaven." This verse seems to be saying that all you need to do in order to get God to do what you want, is to get someone to think the same as you. Imagine if that were true! It's not. The key is the word 'agree'. We only have one word for agree which means to think the same but Jesus meant a very different kind of agreement. The Greek word used in the original is *sumphoneo*, which is much more the kind of agreement that a piccolo might have with a trombone in the context of a symphony orchestra. The picture is that if you are being all that God created you to be and not adapting your responses to sound like mine, and if I'm being all I am created to be and not trying to say what I think you want me to say, then we really have the chance together to discern God's will. We understand the will of God from his Word, through his Spirit, and in fellowship.

The cost of fellowship

There is a danger that we can develop an idealized picture of fellowship as finding 'soul mates' who will help quell the dark ache of loneliness that we all carry with us. Fellowship will not take the pain away. In fact fellowship will focus the pain and force you to confront it. One of the most helpful books on fellowship that I have read is Community and Growth by Jean Vanier. Vanier isn't just talking theoretically about community; he established the L'Arche communities that care for the disabled, so his writing comes from experience. Vanier points out that as you start to be honest, and lift the metaphorical 'mask' that has kept you safe, you actually discover that "community can be a terrible place, because it is a place of relationship; it is the revelation of our wounded emotions and of how painful it can be to live with others, especially with some people. It's so much easier to live with books and objects, television, or dogs and cats! It is so much easier to live alone and just do things for others, when one feels like it."[112]

I have already said that in order to take on any mission, in order to glorify God, you will need to care. The obvious truth is that in order to have fellowship you will also need to take the risk of deeply caring. In deeply caring though, you are opening yourself to the possibility of getting hurt.

Sociologist Willard Waller contended that there was an inverse relationship between love and power. He called this insight the "principle of least interest." Waller contended that in any relationship, the person who has the most personal power exercises the least amount of love, the person who loves the most has the least personal power."[113] Here again we see that the way of love, the way of fellowship is the way of the cross. When you truly love someone, you hand them power to affect you. If you want to limit people's affect on you, the only real way to do that is by withholding love, and as Waller points out, in withholding love from others you also limit your ability to receive love.

A real test of fellowship is what happens when someone lets the team down, and does cause pain, particularly when it is a person people trust. In

Growing Leaders, James Lawrence makes the assertion that the space to fail is actually a fundamental part of an environment in which people can grow. He says, "Love is the defining mark of Christian community (John 13:34-35), forgiveness is the natural result of love. If forgiveness is not part of our culture, we will restrict growth in leadership and discipleship. Leaders grow when they know they can make mistakes and not be thrown out. The defining moment for a church or organisation is not when things are going well, but when their leaders let them down or make a mistake. How will we respond at that moment?"[114] Commitment to fellowship is a commitment to forgiveness.

Fellowship also takes time. To build real fellowship means being with people in the mission but also in other ways and other contexts. If the only conversations you ever engage in are work related, you will find that you will spend your whole life working with strangers. Fellowship requires spending time with people without an agenda, to be with them instead of to do with them. Actually taking time to sit down with people over a meal, on a walk, in a car or anywhere else where the conversation can wander, is an essential part of building the kind of relationships that can cope with the weight of honesty. Some of my favourite times in both Hobart and Victoria, were the conversations over cups of coffee where we were free just to be honest, or the times when we would just 'hang out' and talk about whatever came to mind. It is amazing how often new thoughts came in these moments.

To love a person in such a way that they experience it as love, is one of the most difficult things a human being can do. Eugene Peterson points out: "Love is the most context-specific act in the entire spectrum of human behaviour. There is no other single human act more dependent on, and immersed in, immediate context. A dictionary is nearly worthless in understanding and practising love. Acts of love cannot be canned and then used off the shelf. Every act of love requires creative and personal giving, responding and serving appropriate to – context specific to – both the person doing the loving and the person being loved."[115] Despite all the difficulties, we know in our bones that we were created to be in loving relationships. We know we need fellowship.

As I have already pointed out, Jesus told us[116] that it will be the quality of our life together that will be the proof we are his disciples. Fellowship was one of the standout features of the early church and their life together was attractive. Acts 2:44-47 says "All the believers were together and had everything in common. They sold property and possessions to give to anyone who had need. Every day they continued to meet together in the temple courts. They broke bread in their homes and ate together with glad and sincere hearts, praising God and enjoying the favour of all the people. And the Lord added to their number daily those who were being saved." I love the throwaway line in there, "enjoying the favour of all the people". When we are in fellowship, we won't always be conscious of it, but people will like what they see. People will be attracted, not by our clever programs, wonderful theology or nice buildings. People will be attracted if we are prepared to do the hard yards of fellowship.

We need it

Fellowship is essential to the life of the Kingdom Cell, but it doesn't just happen by itself. I am convinced that it comes almost naturally from a mature love for Jesus and a commitment to a mission. Without those two ingredients fellowship in itself can become an idol. Whenever the church has grown, there has been deep fellowship at the core between people who are committed to Christ, committed to a mission and committed to each other.

11

Leadership and Fellowship

One of the things that may catch you by surprise is that as you open yourself to Jesus and choose a mission, you start to know where you are going. As you start opening yourself to others, you will start to notice that people are watching you, and some will start to follow you. Whether you like it or not, you are leading.

The Bible does indicate that leadership is a spiritual gift,[117] and there has been a lot written and taught about the importance of leadership. The truth is, though, that leadership is quite simple; there are two things necessary: knowing where you are going, and loving people. One of the dangers in the intense focus on leadership in our modern culture is that we raise a whole lot of people who want to be leaders but don't know where they are going and don't love people. I have no doubt that there is a gift of leadership, and that some will be able to more clearly articulate a direction and motivate people to go there than others. However if J. Oswald Sanders is right and "leadership is influence"[118] then we all at some level must lead if we want to influence the world, our communities, our businesses, our churches or our families.

A Kingdom Cell is not a hierarchical structure. In many ways, just like the disciples, the nucleus of a Kingdom Cell is a group of leaders who are looking to empower other leaders. There may be some, like Peter, who are 'first among equals', but in the same way that Paul challenged Peter, no-one in a Kingdom Cell would see themselves as above anyone else. Kingdom Cells rely on servant leadership.

There will be times when, despite having fellowship, carrying the load that God has for you will be a lonely experience. A. W. Tozer wrote "Most of the world's greatest souls have been lonely."[119] J. Oswald Sanders writes, "The leader must be a person who, while welcoming the friendship and support of all who offer it, has sufficient inner resources to stand alone – even in the face of stiff opposition to have 'no one but God.'"[120] While Sander's statement is directed at people who would call themselves leaders, it is also true for all of us who would are committed to seeing the Kingdom come on earth as it is in heaven. There will times where you will need to stand and be counted, perhaps even against the people you would see as your closest friends. Wilberforce stood against Pitt, Paul stood against Barnabas. Fellowship will not mean you will never be on your own.

One of my favourite parts of the movie *Invictus* is an argument that Nelson Mandela (played by Morgan Freeman) has with his assistant about the renaming of the Springboks rugby team. His assistant warns him that he is risking alienating the cabinet, the party and the majority of the people. Mandela's response is "Yes I know but in this instance the people are wrong and as their elected leader it is my job to show them that." When his assistant responds by warning him that he is risking his own future, he says "The day I am afraid to do that is the day I am no longer fit to lead." We will all have moments when it will be necessary to stand against the tide and whether we stand or whether we avoid taking a stand, these are the moments that will define our lives. While this is absolutely true, standing on your own cannot be the pattern all the time, and if it is there is probably something wrong.

Somebody who gains the moral weight we were talking about in the chapter on mission needs fellowship just as much, and probably more, than anyone else. Even Jesus, who was the only human who could lay claim to perfection, sought fellowship in the midst of personal crisis. I have no way of comprehending just how painful Gethsemane was for Jesus, but in that moment we see him longing for company: "He took Peter and the two sons of Zebedee along with him, and he began to be sorrowful and troubled. Then he said to them, 'My soul is overwhelmed with sorrow to the point of death. Stay here and keep watch with me.' Going a little farther, he fell with his face to the ground and prayed, 'My Father, if it is possible, may this cup be taken from me. Yet not as I will, but as you will.' Then he returned to his disciples and found them sleeping. 'Couldn't you men keep watch with me for one hour?' he asked Peter."[121]

If Jesus sought fellowship, it follows that even the best and the brightest of us will need it too. Fellowship, for those who are seen to be significant, is a choice to be vulnerable. Jean Vanier points out, "Good leaders are aware of both their strengths and weaknesses. They are not afraid to admit to the latter. They know how to find support and are humble enough to ask for it. There is no perfect leader who has all the gifts necessary for good leadership."[122]

Unfortunately, when it comes to choosing who to follow, we generally look for someone who might have all the answers. We look for the bright stars, the brilliant performers, the people who seem to be able to do everything.

Since 2006 I have carried around in the back of my Bible an article with the heading "Pastor admits lies and sin."[123] It is a story about Ted Haggard, one of the most significant leaders of the evangelical church in America who made some huge mistakes. I carry it around for two reasons: firstly as a reminder that we are all in danger of being idiots, and secondly as a reminder that we all should be admitting lies and sin a whole lot more than we do. I do not want to justify what Haggard did at all, but I do want to point out that none of us are perfect. The fact that a pastor admitting lies and sin makes headlines says something serious about what we expect of leaders. We are all liars and sinners.

I certainly don't agree with everything Carl Jung wrote, however his statement "The brighter the persona, the darker the shadow," rings very true. After growing up amongst many of the brightest stars in the Australian Christian church, and then spending a number of years on both commercial and Christian radio where I was able to interview many 'stars', I firmly believe that Jung's statement is worthy of consideration. In many ways Paul confirms Jung's thesis when he talks about how magnificent a vision God gave him, and yet, "…in order to keep me from becoming conceited, I was given a thorn in my flesh, a messenger of Satan, to torment me. Three times I pleaded with the Lord to take it away from me."[124] Numerous people have had theories about what Paul's thorn was, but I'm glad he didn't tell us as it makes it easier for me to identify with him. The more I relate to people, the more I believe we all have at least one "thorn in the flesh."

What I understand the idea of the "thorn in the flesh" to mean was captured by an episode of 'The West Wing' where Leo McGarry (played by John Spencer) tries to explain what it means to be an alcoholic and drug addict to a young woman who has tipped the press to his problems. When she asks him how long it took him to be cured he replies, "I'm not cured. You don't get cured. I haven't had a drink or a pill in six and a half years, which isn't to say I won't have one tomorrow."[125] She clearly doesn't understand what he is saying so asks him whether he could possibly have one drink. Leo explains that the problem is that he doesn't want one drink he wants ten drinks, and when she asks why, he just says "'Cause I'm an alcoholic."[126]

I have often quoted this transaction because it captures so well the idea that alcoholics can put themselves in a place where they are powerless in the face of their addiction. It may not be addiction to drugs or alcohol, but as I have spoken to many, many people, I am convinced that we <u>all</u> have our 'thorns in the flesh'. For all of us there are particular circumstances where our ability to make choices is severely inhibited. Those circumstances are different for different people, but the general truth remains.

It is a normal thing to want to minimize pain and maximize pleasure, which is one of the main drives of the flesh. For most of us though, as a result of a mixture of chemical pre-disposition and habits resulting from unhelpful choices, we develop ways of avoiding pain or seeking pleasure that are unhelpful and take us away from the calling God has for us. These coping strategies become 'thorns in the flesh' when instead of choices they become impulses. You know you have a thorn when you can imagine a situation where you no longer have a choice but to act in a way that is damaging for yourself or others. Alcoholism, drugs, eating disorders, gambling and pornography are common thorns and are often spoken about in churches, but there are many others, some of which are less obvious. Computer gaming is fast becoming a major addiction, particularly for males under 35, and immersive games like *Half Life* or *World of Warcraft* give people who feel powerless in the real world an addictive sense of potency in a fictional one. The 2009 movie, *Confessions of a Shopaholic*, highlighted the challenge for some people of coping through spending. Gossip can be a coping strategy for people who generally feel too powerless to take the biblical path to coping with conflict and they can become like a cancer within any group of people.

Paul hated his thorn in the flesh, and was desperate for God to take it away, just as most people who find themselves trapped in reflexive destructive responses feel trapped and desperate for a way out. In 2 Corinthians 12:8-9, he tells us of a response from God that was perhaps not one we would expect. "But he said to me, 'My grace is sufficient for you, for my power is made perfect in weakness.' Therefore I will boast all the more gladly about my weaknesses, so that Christ's power may rest on me." God reminds Paul that his humanity, his weakness, is a critical part of his discipleship. Pride is the most deadly 'thorn in the flesh' of all, because if you fall into the trap of believing you are the centre of the universe, there is no need for God. We all have weaknesses, and it's tempting to look down on people who have different weaknesses than you, but when you do that, you are stepping in to dangerous territory.

There are three key responses to our 'thorns in the flesh' that are signs of maturity. The first and most critical one is to be able to admit, like Paul, that you are not perfect and that you have weaknesses. Once you can do that, you can start to know the grace of God who is not asking you to be perfect. The second response is to identify situations where the thorn is most difficult to manage, and do your best not to be in those situations. The third, and possibly the most challenging in our culture, is to be honest with people you trust so that they can know what signs to be watching for when you are not coping. This level of fellowship is essential for everyone, and particularly for leaders.

Imagine a world where you didn't feel you could make mistakes! Unfortunately some of us live in a world where we think that is what is expected of us. We aim for perfection without wanting to acknowledge our own personal sin. Eugene Peterson points out: "This is why perfectionists so often become workaholics; by ignoring the ubiquity of sin they persist in the illusion that if they accomplish just one more mission, master just one more act of devotion, successfully avoid contamination with just one more sloppily living Christian, get one more program up and running, they will emerge head and shoulders above all others. Some of them accomplish impressive projects and manage stunning achievements, but they also end up without friends, often without family, without forgiveness because they never need it, and without love."[127]

In *The Leadership Secrets of Billy Graham*, authors Harold Myra and Marshall Shelly, recount a moment when Billy called together his team and wrestled together about the number of Christian ministries that were being destroyed when leaders made serious mistakes.[128] They agreed that they would work on keeping each other accountable in four distinct areas: money, relationships with the opposite sex, speaking badly of other ministries and exaggerating the accomplishments of their ministry. This pact of Graham's senior leaders was actually taken extremely seriously, to the point where they made sure they travelled together and no-one was left at a hotel alone. I don't think it is an overstatement to say that the stability of Billy Graham's historic ministry was a direct result of that very personal pact.

Keeping one another on track is a much easier thing to do in a Kingdom Cell, where you are seeing one another regularly and have a shared goal and values, than in almost any other structure. If you are still on the journey to find others who are called to a similar mission to you, please don't use that as an excuse for failing to find fellowship and accountability. Finding people you can trust is not always easy, but not finding them can cause much more damage in the long term.

As you open yourself to Jesus and accept a mission from him, you will gradually notice that pressure begins to build. Satan has an investment in stopping you. Someone who is in community, who is able to admit their own weaknesses and who has people committed to keeping them accountable is much less likely to stumble and fall in the face of that building pressure. All of us, and particularly people who are seen as having moral authority, need this kind of fellowship.

12

The Fourth Radical Decision: Hospitality

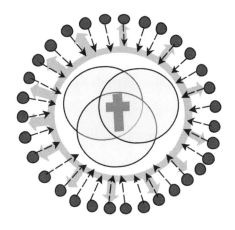

Have you ever met someone fresh out of Bible College? They are usually full of right ideas and full of themselves.

As I look back, that's certainly what I was like in 1992. A fellow graduate and I stood on the bow of the boat taking us down to our placements in Tasmania and engaged in a serious discussion about what we would do in three years time, after we had transformed Tasmania. Needless to say we both quickly discovered that life is more complicated that you can ever fully grasp in a classroom.

A few days after arriving in Hobart I met George. I had grand plans and was reading all I could about being an effective leader. George came into the office and didn't say much, he just gave me a hug. I was dumbstruck.

George, I found out, was a regular visitor to different churches and Christian organisations where he did the same thing. He asked me what my plans were, and after I told him I was going to change Tasmania he smiled and told me that God gave him the ministry of loving people and giving them hugs.

I saw George regularly over the next years, and as my plans gradually unravelled, my appreciation for George increased. George saw lots of enthusiastic people come into ministries in Hobart, and many disillusioned ones leave. He loved them all. At times when I felt I no longer had any answers, George would often turn up with remarkable timing and offer to pray for me. Gradually I learned that real ministry was about how you treated people, and not so much about grand plans.

It is clear that we are called to be hospitable:

> "Share with the Lord's people who are in need. Practice hospitality."
> *(Romans 12:13)*

> "Do not forget to show hospitality to strangers, for by so doing some people have shown hospitality to angels without knowing it."
> *(Hebrews 13:2)*

> "Offer hospitality to one another without grumbling." *(1 Peter 4:9)*

In both Timothy and Titus, being hospitable is one of the key qualifications for church leadership. It is absolutely clear that hospitality was one of the key ingredients in the explosion of the New Testament church. Hospitality too, was central to the way that Basil's monks lived their lives, it was at the heart of the Wesleyan movement and the Moravian movement. In fact as far as I can tell whenever God is moving, his people are welcoming the stranger.

So if hospitality is so important, why are there so many lonely people in our communities and even in our churches?

Seven years ago I moved with my family to the Mornington Peninsula, just outside of Melbourne. I'm fairly sure the reason God took us to Mornington was to teach me about hospitality. We moved into a four bedroom flat that was part of an old officer's mess, the only building left from an army camp that used to cover the Balcombe estate. Alongside our flat there was another family living in a two bedroom flat and seventeen bedrooms upstairs where single members of the team lived as well as up to six homeless young people at any one time. Because the community was so confined and intense it served as a laboratory in which we would get very direct feedback. Whenever the young people felt seen and valued, Balcombe was a beautiful, rewarding and enriching place to be. When we started getting too busy for them, pre-occupied or focused too much on rules and regulations, Balcombe quickly became a living hell.

I learned a lot from the young people who lived with us in those five years. I realised my natural tendency is to be pre-occupied, and I am sad to say that there were a number of young people who lived under the same roof as me, who I never actually got to know. There was one young person in particular who taught me a profound lesson. His name too, was Matt.

Matt, like most of the young people who came to stay with us, had a complex background. He obviously identified with the hip-hop sub-culture and enjoyed playing his music very loudly, which was a challenge because his bedroom was directly above ours. After some initial challenges, he started to settle in and became attached to my children. Moving into an intense community like this with my family was not an easy decision. Leeanne and I talked at length about the risks and prayed regularly for safety. Looking back I can see God looked after us. I can also see clearly that often the Garvin kids were the best youth workers in the building. Both my sons would have long discussions with Matt about all kinds of things, and Matt seemed to instinctively change his behaviour whenever he saw Maddi, Josh, Daniel or Sophie anywhere near him. I still remember the Christmas when he knocked on the door and rather sheepishly offered presents for each one of my children. He had taken the time to think of each one and tried to find something that would bring joy to them.

Matt travelled with Fusion to Tasmania for a one week *Youth Foundations* course and through the process welcomed Jesus into his life. It became clear that Matt was ready to leave the Balcombe community, and he was keen to start to stand on his own two feet. He would still drop in regularly though, and in particular would ring one of our team members, Chris, who had become a bit like a surrogate dad for him. Chris played that role for lots of the young people mainly because of all our team he was the one who gave them the most space.

I still remember getting the devastating phone call telling me Matt was in a coma.

A month or so earlier he had applied for an apprenticeship as a truck mechanic, something he had set his heart on. Two out of three of the business owners had said yes, but one said no and that hurt Matt. He lost focus and direction, and when a next door neighbour offered him drugs, he couldn't resist. He went into a coma and a short while later he died. It was a sad funeral. Matt had so much to offer, and yet he was gone. Matt had been a gift to me. I saw something of his spirit in the way he connected with my children and the way he wanted to tackle life head on. What I had to face though was that while it's easy to blame a business owner, I could have made the space to know what that interview had meant for Matt. I could have created the space to talk the rejection through with him. I could have been hospitable to Matt at a time when he most needed it. The real reason I wasn't was that I was too busy. I was too full of the rest of my agenda, my plans, my family, my television, and my dreams. I didn't create the space Matt needed. He stands as a symbol for me of why creating space is so important: if one person had created just a little more space, Matt may still be alive today.

In his book, *Reaching Out*, Henri Nouwen defines hospitality as "primarily the creation of a free space where the stranger can enter and become a friend instead of an enemy. Hospitality is not to change people, but to offer them space where change can take place."[129] He goes on to say that "The paradox of hospitality is that it wants to create emptiness, not a fearful emptiness, but a friendly emptiness where strangers can enter and discover themselves as created free; free to sing their own songs, speak their own languages, dance their own dances; free also to leave and follow their own vocations. Hospitality is not a subtle invitation to adopt the life style of the host, but the gift of a chance for the guest to find his own."[130]

Hospitality requires a fundamental willingness to be open to different ways of seeing the world. It requires openness to people with different value systems and different life experiences. Hospitality is deeply confronting. To truly see transformation we need to be ready to step outside of the neat and tidy world we have created for ourselves. Nouwen says "Really honest receptivity means inviting the stranger into our world on his or her terms, not on ours. When we say, 'You can be my guest if you believe what I believe, think the way I think and behave as I do', we offer love under a condition or for a price. This leads easily to exploitation, making hospitality into a business."[131]

Being hospitable actually means a loss of control, intentionally allowing other people to influence how you spend your time. Nouwen quotes a professor from the University of Notre Dame as saying, "You know . . . my whole life I have been complaining that my work was constantly interrupted, until I discovered that my interruptions were my work."[132]

Conflict and hospitality

Through the many different experiences I have had of Christians trying to live together in community, I have come to the surprising understanding that hospitality is as much about conflict as it is about space.

A lot of conflict comes from miscommunication. When you use a particular phrase, or screw up your nose in a particular way, you may be meaning something completely different than I would if I used the same phrase or screwed up my nose in that way. When we first meet, I don't know that. When you speak to me I assume that you mean what I would mean if I said what you were saying. The thing is, you almost never do.

One of the most intense parts of Fusion's training has been the Group Life Laboratory. Bennis and Shepherd, who dreamed up the exercise in the 1970s, point out that real communication in a group can only happen once people go through the pain of realising they see the world differently.[133] What they were saying was that valid communication only starts to happen when I start to understand what you mean by your words and your actions, and you start to understand what I mean by my words and my actions.

Effective communication requires commitment and skill, and even then one of the phrases Fusion trainers most often use is, "intention doesn't guarantee performance". Just because you want to communicate doesn't mean you will. Two of the most important things to master if you hope to relate effectively to people are the skill of empathic listening and the skill of honest feedback. Nobody is born naturally good at either listening or feedback, both skills require an effort to put aside self interest and deeply engage with another person.

Conflict is not always the result of miscommunication. Risking conflict is actually a critical part of real hospitality. I still remember coming across the couple of sentences from Henri Nouwen four months into my placement in Hobart. I was feeling disillusioned because it felt like there was lots of stuff going on under the surface amongst our team, yet no-one would say anything. I had tried all my theories from the training and they didn't seem to be working, gradually as I read what Nouwen was saying, I saw that the theories were not the issue, it was me. I had to start letting people know what was going on for me.

Nouwen puts it like this: "…receptivity is only one side of hospitality. The other side, equally important, is confrontation. To be receptive to the stranger in no way implies that we have to become neutral 'nobodies'. Real receptivity asks for confrontation because space can only be a welcoming space when there are clear boundaries, and boundaries are limits between which we define our own position. Flexible limits, but limits none the less. Confrontation results from the articulate presence, the presence within boundaries, of the host to the guest by which he offers himself as a point of orientation and a frame of reference."[134]

What Nouwen is saying is that it's not enough to work hard at creating space for people; they actually have to get to know you if you want to be hospitable. They need to know what you care about, what you hope, what you fear. They also need to know your boundaries. They need to know what kind of behaviour you feel comfortable with and what kind of behaviour you feel uncomfortable with. You have to be ready to be what Nouwen calls a "*point of orientation or a frame of reference.*"[135] When George came into my life, he became a point of orientation for me. I am sad that I was not more of a point of orientation for Matt.

The apostle Paul understood the importance of becoming a frame of reference for others. He advises Titus in chapter 2:7 that his job is to allow people to watch him: "And you yourself must be an example to them by doing good deeds of every kind. Let everything you do reflect the integrity and seriousness of your teaching."

Peter also advises that the job of a leader is to be a point of orientation: "Care for the flock of God entrusted to you. Watch over it willingly, not grudgingly—not for what you will get out of it, but because you are eager to serve God. Don't lord it over the people assigned to your care, but lead them by your good example."[136]

At the start of his journey with the disciples, Jesus sat them down in Matthew 10 and spelt out to them what the adventure would entail.

I first started to register the significance of the chapter in reading *the Message* paraphrase by Eugene Petersen, and verses 5 to 10 leapt off the page. Jesus sent his twelve harvest hands out with this charge: "Don't begin by travelling to some far-off place to convert unbelievers. And don't try to be dramatic by tackling some public enemy. Go to the lost, confused people right here in the neighbourhood. Tell them that the kingdom is here. Bring health to the sick. Raise the dead. Touch the untouchables. Kick out the demons. You have been treated generously, so live generously. Don't think you have to put on a fund-raising campaign before you start. You don't need a lot of equipment. You are the equipment, and all you need to keep that going is three meals a day. Travel light."

I unpack Matthew 10 more fully in my book *Faith Reflections*,[137] but this passage has particular relevance to the question of what it means to reach out beyond ourselves. Jesus introduces the idea that mission is not a big plan or program, rather it is about connecting with the people in front of your face, it is local and it is relational. He also makes it clear that mission is a response to the love of God, not something we do for God. I love the way Petersen puts it, "You have been treated generously, so live generously." Too often we 'professional' Christians can turn it on for a training seminar, a sermon or a mission program and then want our space so we can be ourselves again. Jesus is saying that the programs and speaking are nowhere near as important as being generous with your life.

As a leader of a Christian mission organisation I found what Jesus says next quite confronting: "Don't think you have to put on a fund-raising campaign before you start. You don't need a lot of equipment. You are the equipment." It's easy to fall into a trap of thinking that the work you do is the important bit of ministry, but Jesus makes it clear that it's not about the plans or the programs – it's about you. As I started to come to terms with this small-scale, dirty-hands Christianity I realised how different this approach was from how many people, including myself, were seeing mission.

13

Hospitality and Mission

Understanding hospitality reframes our understanding of mission. Often mission is seen as something we do, a program we run, a church service we invite people to, or a speech we give.

A normal approach to ministry or social work is to look for people with a problem that you can help them solve. Even if that problem is the absence of a relationship with Jesus Christ, this approach inherently comes from a point of view, "I'm ok but you're not ok and if you listen to me I will make you ok." Kingdom Cells are different. Instead of seeing people as clients, outsiders are invited inside.

When a Kingdom Cell is alive, discovering Jesus happens as people encounter each other, as people let their lives do the communicating rather than any technique or program.

In 2005, as the Fusion team in Victoria were preparing for the influx of people from around the world to participate in training and mission for the Commonwealth Games, God gave us a passage of Scripture that framed the way we approached the event: "Enlarge the place of your tent, stretch your tent curtains wide, do not hold back; lengthen your cords, strengthen your stakes. For you will spread out to the right and to the left; your descendants will dispossess nations and settle in their desolate cities."[138]

That passage asked a few key questions of us. The first question was *'Are we willing to welcome people into where we live?'* For the writer of Isaiah your tent was your home, and making it bigger and opening the door wide meant inviting people into your life, not just into your program. A good place to start is to look at your diary and at your house and ask, *"Is there actually room for others?"* If not, make room. Leeanne has deliberately organized our little house so hospitality is easier. We have a sofa bed in the lounge room and also out in the shed that functions as my study. We have dining room table that can seat four extra places beyond our family of six and we have seating in our lounge room for ten.

The second question was *'Would we deliberately expand our capacity to welcome people in?'* Expanding the tent, opening the curtains wide and lengthening the cords are all about being prepared to grow, even before the people turn up. I am grateful for some of the structures in our village that help create the space for hospitality. Each week we have a "community tea" where different people come round to our house for tea. We also have a morning tea each week day where we have the chance to connect briefly and informally.

The third question was *'Are we grounded enough in what really matters?'* The picture of strengthening your stakes is one of nailing down the foundation points so that the added strain of a bigger tent doesn't mean the whole thing will collapse. One of the dangers of welcoming people in is that they come with all their histories and different ideas, and unless the foundational truth of who you are is very secure, it is likely to collapse. The more you expand, the stronger the stakes need to be.

The New Testament church welcomed people into their homes; they made a practice of hospitality, and because of that they needed to find a way to hang on to the foundational truths. A number of the epistles were written specifically to help them know what it meant to 'strengthen their stakes' in the face of new ideas and teaching that was taking them off the track.

We have to remember though that it's not physically possible to have space for all the hurting people in your life. Even Jesus didn't deeply connect with every person he came into contact with. I am convinced though, that it is real hospitality, the creation of space for others, which is actually at the heart of any situation where God's people are changing the world. As I look at some of the most effective things the Christian church does, the core is not a great performance or a clever program, it is hospitality. The genius of the Alpha course is not the wonderful teaching but the creation of a safe space for dialogue. Fusion's Open Crowd Festivals have been so effective because they are simply a way to be hospitable to a whole community.[139]

When people connect to a Kingdom Cell, they receive the benefit of connection to the life of Jesus Christ. They feel loved and respected, challenged and encouraged. They are provoked to be more the person they were created to be. No wonder a Kingdom Cell can have such an impact! We need to get used to the idea that our lives rather than our programs, tracts or speeches are what draw people to connect.

Hospitality for the poor

The Bible makes it clear that there is a particular group of people that we all need to care for. In the Old Testament, over and over again, the prophets would ask about three groups of people: the widows, the orphans and the strangers. In today's language they were asking about the single mothers, the homeless kids and the refugees. Why the focus on these three groups? The prophets were asking about the weakest members of the community. The clearest measure of how justice and love are going in any community is how the weakest, poorest and most isolated are being cared for.

As Bono points out, "The one thing on which we can all agree, among all faiths and ideologies, is that God is with the vulnerable and poor. God is in the slums, in the cardboard boxes where the poor play house. God is in the silence of a mother who has infected her child with a virus that will end both their lives. God is in the cries heard under the rubble of war. God is in the debris of wasted opportunity and lives, and God is with us if we are with them."[140]

In every society, in fact in every group, there is someone on the bottom of the status ladder. God wants us to create space for those people who others often overlook. I love the rallying cry that founder of the Salvation Army, William Booth, gave "While women weep, as they do now, I'll fight; while children go hungry, as they do now I'll fight; while men go to prison, in and out, in and out, as they do now, I'll fight; while there is a drunkard left, while there is a poor lost girl upon the streets, while there remains one dark soul without the light of God, I'll fight, I'll fight to the very end!"[141]

The outcome of any Kingdom Cell's commitment to hospitality will be that life for the poor, the weak, the oppressed will be better. Ronald J. Sider, in *The Scandal of Evangelical Conscience*, quoted both Richard Lovelace and J. Edwinn Orr, "both evangelical historians of revival movements, [who] point out that evangelism and concern for the poor, have gone hand in hand in the great revivals of the past."[142]

So what does this mean?

Mission or evangelism happens naturally when the Kingdom Cell is alive and well, and it is in danger of being a waste of time when it is not. When a small group of friends commit to the revolutionary act of wholeheartedly loving Jesus, and as a result, loving one another and loving their neighbours, the life that is created naturally draws people in. If people are not being attracted to you, it's time to look again at the 6 Radical Questions. The Kingdom of God is attractive.

The challenge should not be about finding people, but about being willing to welcome them in. The real question that faces a Kingdom Cell is, *are its members willing for the small group to become a bigger group?* At one level that question seems obvious, and many churches are crying out for more people. However more people bring more problems, personalities and ideas with them. Are we really willing to change and adapt to accommodate the different personalities and gifts that God brings? The problem with welcoming the stranger is that they are, well, strange!

It was clear that the early church had numerous difficulties that arose from welcoming people in. Chapters 12 and 13 of 1 Corinthians were written particularly to address the challenges of loving one another despite differences. Romans 14:1 also couldn't be much clearer: "Welcome with open arms fellow believers who don't see things the way you do. And don't jump all over them every time they do or say something you don't agree with—even when it seems that they are strong on opinions but weak in the faith department. Remember, they have their own history to deal with. Treat them gently."[143]

For a true Kingdom Cell, finding people will never be your problem. The problem will be what you do with them when they want to connect. A willingness to welcome people into our lives, deliberately expanding our capacity, and a deep commitment to the foundational truth of who we are, are the three essential ingredients of hospitality.

14

The Fifth Radical Decision: Empowerment

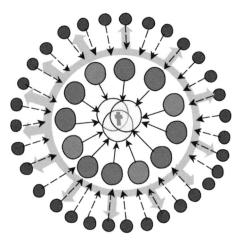

At the end of his autobiography, Nelson Mandela wrote the words "For to be free is not merely to cast off one's chains, but to live in a way that respects and enhances the freedom of others."[144]

On Robben Island, where Mandela was imprisoned for so many years, I started to understand just what his words meant. I met a man that I consider great. He was our tour guide, I couldn't quite understand his name, and I was too embarrassed to ask him to repeat it. I wish I had.

Trying to make conversation I asked him whether he enjoyed doing the tour. His response was immediate "No – it's depressing".Yet he still shows up. His expensive footwear and clothing were an indication he wasn't here for the money. His friends are now running the country.

He took us to his cell and showed us the menu that was segregated so that "Asiatics" got better treatment than blacks. He matter of factly told us about his ongoing kidney and liver issues from the only avenue of protest open to the prisoners – hunger strikes. At the end of the tour he sat us down and asked for questions. He had successfully avoided telling much of his own story to that point, so I asked him how he ended up on the island. He told a brief story of a young idealist who got involved in the student movement, stole across the border to Angola to receive military training and came back to the struggle in Soweto before being arrested at the age of 24. I remembered what I was like at that age and tried to imagine how I would cope with the hard labour and inhuman treatment of the island. I couldn't imagine it.

As the boat pulled away I was challenged both by the humility of this man and his commitment to persevere through suffering. Every day since 2005 he makes the trip back to the island, confronting his horrible memories for the sake of people like me. People who might only hear of apartheid in books or on television. People who might let it happen again unless they are confronted with the stark, brutal reality of what one man can do to another. As a young man he was ready to fight, as an older man he realises his job is to help others join the battle.

We all want to be free, but as Nelson Mandela points out; freedom carries with it a responsibility that we tend not to want to examine. True freedom enhances the freedom of others. Discovering a personal relationship with Jesus actually leads you to finding your own voice, as does accepting a mission, real fellowship and hospitality. All of these things lead you towards freedom, but that freedom then comes with the responsibility to empower others.

Empowerment is a word that has been used in many circles and while the general sense is the same, the actual idea is a challenging one to nail down. The author of a report called *Entry points for Empowerment* says, "Empowerment is like the taste of mango, or the scent of jasmine, or the sound of the waves on the shore; almost everybody can recognize those things for what they are, but almost nobody can describe them."[145] The dictionary[146] says that to empower someone is to enable them, to give them influence or to promote their self actualisation.

Self actualisation was a term made popular by Abraham Maslow and he placed it at the top of his hierarchy of human needs. For Maslow, the term meant "The drive to become what one is capable of being." The idea assumes that we all have a "potential self," that we are capable of becoming. Not everyone would agree with that idea, but it is very much a biblical one. From the first couple of chapters, the Bible is absolutely clear that we humans are unique on the earth because we are created in the image of God. When God breathed life into man,[147] it was an action of creation quite different from the creation of every other living thing. In both Hebrew and Greek, the word for breath and for spirit is the same word.[148] As God gave us life, he gave us a spirit, and the human quest is the quest to live with integrity, to live in a way that is true to the part that is created in the image of God.

When Steve Jobs died, I was surprised about the level of grief that swept the world. I was in South Africa at the time and I read article after article about Jobs legacy. The thing that touched me most however, came from the man himself. In 2005, Stanford University had invited Steve to deliver their commencement speech, and what he delivered was an outstanding example of the power of communication. As he brought the speech to a close, Jobs challenged the audience directly: "Your time is limited, so don't waste it living someone else's life. Don't be trapped by dogma — which is living with the results of other people's thinking. Don't let the noise of others' opinions drown out your own inner voice. And most important, have the courage to follow your heart and intuition. They somehow already know what you truly want to become. Everything else is secondary."[149]

We all have what Steve Jobs calls "heart and intuition", what the Bible calls the spirit. The young Elihu, says in Job 32:8 "But it is the spirit in a person, the breath of the Almighty, that gives them understanding." Both Steve Jobs and the book of Job are talking about a different way of 'knowing'; a knowing that comes from somewhere other than the head. Romans 8:16 indicates that it is our spirits, and not our brains, that are central in how we relate to God: "The Spirit himself testifies with our spirit that we are God's children."

One of my favourite things to do is to teach Fusion's students the book of Ecclesiastes. Professor Peter Kreeft says "Ecclesiastes is the one book in the Bible that modern man needs most to read, for it is Lesson One, and the rest of the Bible is Lesson Two, and modernity does not heed Lesson Two because it does not heed Lesson One."[150] After spending a couple of years wrestling with the book, I agree wholeheartedly with Professor Kreeft. Ecclesiastes is remarkable because it dares to ask the question "Is there any point to life?" Rather than just settle for a simple clichéd response, the book chronicles the journey of someone looking for fulfilment in places that sound quite familiar to the modern ear. The teacher[151] tries to find meaning in thinking, in pleasure, in beautiful houses and food, in work, in relationships and in all the normal ways we human beings try to find fulfilment today. After each attempt he dismisses the particular path with the summary statement that it was meaningless, often with the additional phrase "a chasing after the wind."

The book goes in two arcs, from chapter one to three and then from three to twelve, reaching the same conclusion on both journeys. Coming after the beautiful "time for every purpose" verses that became the basis for a song written by Pete Seeger that was a number one hit for *The Byrds*, Ecclesiastes 3:11 is a key to the whole book. The verse says three important things "He has made everything beautiful in its time. He has also set eternity in the human heart; yet no one can fathom what God has done from beginning to end." Firstly, the teacher builds on the first eight verses of chapter three and points out that there is a right time for everything, and in that time, everything is beautiful. Secondly, he makes the significant statement, "He has also set eternity in the human heart," but he contrasts that with a third statement, "Yet no one can fathom what God has done from beginning to end." Right here we see the human dilemma: there is a beautiful part of all of us, created in the image of God, a part that like Steve Jobs says, "Somehow already know(s) what you truly want to become," but that part of us is beyond our own intellectual understanding.

I love the picture painted in both the gospel of Mark and the gospel of Luke[152] of people bringing their children to meet Jesus. The disciples thought they were about the serious business of the Kingdom of God, but Jesus used the moment to illustrate that they were really missing the point. He calls the kids, and once they are surrounding him he says, "Truly I tell you, anyone who will not receive the kingdom of God like a little child will never enter it."[153] I could never relate to this story until I had my own children and I discovered something over and over again. It is not possible to relate to children and be pre-occupied. A child lives <u>in the moment</u>; we adults tend to live elsewhere: either replaying the past, worrying about the future or in some fantasy. My read of what Jesus is saying is that, *"If you want to be in my Kingdom, you need to be ready to throw away whatever agenda you might have and be in this moment with me."*

The Kingdom of God requires us to be free to respond to find the beautiful time in the current reality in which we find ourselves. Romans 10:17 says "Consequently, faith comes from hearing the message, and the message is heard through the word about Christ." The Greek word for word in this verse is *rhema*, which means God's specific word for this moment. The verse more accurately should read *"faith (is) from hearing, and the hearing through a word of Christ"*[154] To have faith is to be present, with Jesus, in this moment that God has you in. That is much easier said than done, but it is the very essence of the Kingdom of God.

Empowerment in God's Kingdom, is to be free to fulfill our God given potential: to be enabled and free to respond to the moment with integrity, in harmony with God.

15

Disempowerment

If empowering is about enabling, allowing people to influence and helping people fulfill their potential, then disempowerment is about disabling, keeping people quiet and trapping them in unfulfilled lives.

The great challenge in even starting to talk about empowerment is that the only people who can truly empower the powerless are the powerless themselves. As Paulo Friere points out, empowerment requires people who see themselves as oppressed not in a "closed world from which there is no exit, but as a limiting situation which they can transform."[155] Because the assumption at the heart of Christianity is that *Jesus Christ is Lord* over every aspect of life, Christians who actually believe this naturally look at their life circumstance from a position of empowerment. Paul writes "I have learned to be content whatever the circumstances. I know what it is to be in need, and I know what it is to have plenty. I have learned the secret of being content in any and every situation, whether well fed or hungry, whether living in plenty or in want. I can do all this through him who gives me strength."[156]

So the starting point of empowerment, in the Kingdom of God, is to realise that Christ is in us,[157] and as a result we don't have to approach the world as victims of outside forces over which we have no escape. The flipside to that argument though, is that despite the fact we have the one who flung stars into space with us in every moment, we manage to continually sabotage ourselves. It would be interesting to front up to a committee who were looking to employ a Christian leader and say, "I do not understand what I do. For what I want to do I do not do, but what I hate I do."[158] or "I have the desire to do what is good, but I cannot carry it out. For I do not do the good I want to do, but the evil I do not want to do—this I keep on doing."[159] My guess is I wouldn't get the job. I'm glad though that Paul had the courage to be honest, and in his honesty identified one of the main sources of our own disempowerment. As the famous American cartoon said "We have met the enemy and he is us."[160]

So often the main reason we are not fulfilling our potential is that there is quite simply part of us that doesn't want to. It is for this reason, I believe that the New Testament spends so much time talking about the importance of fellowship, and that fellowship is an essential part of a Kingdom Cell. In the dark moments when God feels a long way away and we are ready to give up, we need brothers and sisters who will love us enough not to condemn, but gently remind us who we are capable of being. I love that the word *encourage* comes from the French words *en* (in) and *coeur* (heart), so the word literally means "putting heart into." We need people who will encourage us.

If a major feature of disempowerment is keeping people quiet, then again the biggest factor in that, is us. Charles Templeton, in his book Evangelism for Tomorrow, wrote "The church stands in danger that the time will come when it can pick up a microphone and address the entire world – only to find it has nothing to say."[161] A really important question to ask ourselves, "*Have I got anything worthwhile to say to the world?*" Sometimes the church looks dysfunctional because we respond to complex issues with un-thought-out clichés. As you truly open your life to Christ, and tackle the mission he gives you in fellowship, then real hospitality, openness to the reality facing the people around you, will give you no end of important things to say. Mother Theresa was able to speak with authority because she knew her personal mission, and she was motivated by the realities facing the people she was caring for. The person, who has no purpose in their life and no awareness of others, is unlikely to have anything worthwhile to say. As you know your mission and are welcoming the stranger into your life, nobody will be able to keep you quiet.

16

Platform Builders

While empowerment is something that ultimately comes from our own individual choices, there are things we can do in order to make that journey as simple as possible for others. Jesus makes it clear that we are held responsible if our actions trip another person up, [162] and Paul indicates that we should measure our actions based on the effect they have on others. [163]

Bob Adams was a primary school teacher who left his job because he wanted to live his faith in a way that made a difference for Australian teenagers. There was something different about the way he approached life and relationships. People who met Bob knew that he loved Jesus and loved them. I remember a time I was feeling a bit disheartened during Fusion's training. Bob happened to be a guest lecturer and he pulled me aside and simply said, with tears in his eyes, "Matt I'm proud of you." Those words mattered to a 20 year old who was trying to work out whether leaving a good job in radio was a smart idea after all.

Our main task in the empowerment of others is to create a platform where they are free to discover Christ, find their own mission, find fellowship, be hospitable and empower others. To empower is to be a *platform builder*. When we empower others we create platforms that support them so that they are truly free to discover Christ and their mission in the context of hospitality. In contrast to a ladder, a platform not only gives them stability but it gives boundaries within which people can move with freedom.

A platform, though, does have boundaries, if it truly is to be a platform and not a cliff from which we fall. As I wrote about earlier, there is a basic platform for empowerment that God communicates to Moses on Mount Sinai, and that is the platform of His nature, the Glory of God. As Paul says in Galatians 5:13, we are all free in Christ, but we are not free to do whatever we want. He exhorts us to use our freedom as a platform to "serve one another humbly in love." We are free within the boundaries of justice and love.

Bob Adams built platforms. On one occasion, I walked in on a conversation between my dad, Mal, and Bob as Bob was saying "You can trust him Mal, give Matt a go." Dad saw me out of the corner of his eye and turned and asked whether I would be willing to teach one of the major units in the Foundations mission training course. That moment marked the start of my journey with Bible teaching, and had a significant impact on the course of my life since then. When Bob contracted terminal brain cancer and eventually died, I found it particularly hard because he was someone who had truly seen me. Throughout his life Bob carried a fair bit of self doubt, and would always be quicker to speak about his failures than his successes, however the way that person after person spoke at his funeral about the profound influence Bob had been in their lives, was evidence that Bob created platforms for many, many people.

Bob is someone who continues to be a point of reference in my life. For me, he stands as one of the "great cloud of witnesses" the writer of Hebrews mentions at the start of chapter 12. Every now and then I still wander down to the Poatina memorial garden to have a chat with Bob. I love the idea that all the heroes I have written about in this book are up in the grandstand cheering you and I on in our event, and that someday it will be our turn to be in that grandstand. They helped create a platform for us, and it's our job to create a platform for others.

Barnabas

We are told that Barnabas was sent by the church in Jerusalem to examine what was going on in Antioch. Although it was startling that Gentiles were coming to faith, Barnabas was open enough to God to embrace what was happening.[164] One version of the story says, "As soon as he arrived, he saw that God was behind and in it all. He threw himself in with them, got behind them, urging them to stay with it the rest of their lives. He was a good man that way, enthusiastic and confident in the Holy Spirit's ways. The community grew large and strong in the Master."[165]

The Bible doesn't say what it was at Antioch that got Barnabas thinking that Saul of Tarsus might benefit from being there, but he did, and that tells us a lot about Barnabas. After all it is one thing to be pleased to see God work in the life of an enemy; it is another thing entirely to then want to spend time with them. My guess is that many people in the early church were still suspicious of Saul, who was directly responsible for so much pain and anguish. Even if they believed in his dramatic conversion, the faces of those who had been killed or tortured because of his actions would have been framing their thoughts about the man now called Paul. Barnabas though, saw something in the new believers at Antioch that told him Paul needed to be there, so he travelled to Tarsus to find him.

Acts 11:26 tells us that Barnabas and Paul stayed with the church at Antioch, teaching and connecting with people. My guess is that this year was a bit like Paul's apprenticeship. I can imagine he and Barnabas sitting up late at night having long discussions as Paul applied his brilliant Pharisaic mind to coming to terms with what it meant to live as a Christ follower in this completely foreign setting. I have a sense that this time was formative in terms of Paul's personal mission. Growing up as a Pharisee and the son of a Pharisee, Paul would have been very comfortable with Jewish culture and customs but would have steered away from close contact with the Gentiles.

The year at Antioch would have been almost a cultural exchange for Paul and Barnabas as they saw the Gospel reaching people they would never have thought to engage with previously. Paul came to believe that he had a specific call to the Gentiles, which is a remarkable turnaround for someone from his background. Barnabas was initially like a mentor for Paul, but gradually Paul's influence grew and that of Barnabas diminished. For a period of time Barnabas and Paul travelled and ministered together.

Paul and Barnabas' partnership ends when Paul refuses to welcome Mark back onto the team after he deserted them.[166] Barnabas chooses to stand his ground and fight for the young man. We don't hear a lot more from Barnabas, however we see that he must have done a good job in mentoring Mark because Paul's attitude has changed by the time he writes to Timothy, "Get Mark and bring him with you, because he is helpful to me in my ministry."[167]

Barnabas has a significant ministry in his own right, however; in creating a platform for both Paul and Mark he actually helps to lay the groundwork for the whole Christian movement.

Throughout history, whenever you see God's Kingdom breaking out, the results are far reaching because many, many people are empowered to change the world. When John Wesley had such a radical personal encounter with Jesus, the result was not just a dramatic development of his personal ministry, but a shift in the way Christianity was seen in England more broadly. His action created a climate where people like John Newton, who wrote *Amazing Grace* and the Clapham sect could more readily find their voices. I love the fact that Wesley, who was so busy with his own ministry, had the time and space to encourage, William Wilberforce, who was fighting for the abolition of slavery with his friends from Clapham. Wesley's letter was written to spur Wilberforce to hang on. He wrote something like "unless you are sure God is in this thing then it's better to give up, but we both know He is, and how serious the issue is, so keep going".[168]

The action of Wilberforce and the Clapham sect also resulted in thousands, and perhaps millions, of people being freed to live whole lives. As one historian points out: "They fostered evangelical Christianity; encouraged the Church Missionary Society and the British and Foreign Bible Society; encouraged the good administration of India; encouraged education and backed the Sunday School movement (Robert Raikes); founded Sierra Leone, and Zachary Macaulay put it on its feet; attacked blood sports, duelling and gambling; set higher standards of morality in public life; set higher standards of active concern in politics and abolished the slave trade."

Paul wrote to the Philippians: "Do nothing out of selfish ambition or vain conceit. Rather, in humility value others above yourselves, not looking to your own interests but each of you to the interests of the others."[169] This is not an easy thing to do, but it is the key to long term effectiveness in the Kingdom of God. Former U.S. President, Harry Truman said "You can accomplish anything in life provided you do not mind who gets the credit."[170] Sadly too many of us do care who gets the credit, and we want it to be us.

When a small group of friends begin to seek first the Kingdom of God, they create a platform of justice and love that allows others to find God's purpose for their lives. A clear picture for me of Kingdom platform builders are two chicken farmers, Ian and Jayne Dixon, from the Victorian city of Bendigo. Ian is the quiet, practical type who would much rather be doing something with his hands than speaking to a group of people. Jayne, his wife, loves to look you in the eyes and ask earnestly "So how are you?" She loves people but would be the first to point out that she really is not very confident in her own ability.

In 2004 their church shut down after gradually losing more and more people to the point where it was no longer viable. The members of the church went their separate ways, each finding new spiritual homes, however the building in the Northern suburbs of Bendigo was still there.

Jayne felt deeply that teenagers and young mums in particular needed help so she spoke to the other former members of the church and set out on a quest to invite Fusion to establish a ministry in Bendigo.

By the time that the discussion had got serious, I had just moved to Victoria with my family to head up Fusion's ministry there. It was evident that Ian and Jayne were looking for Fusion to send the experts to address the needs they so clearly saw. As I spoke with them both and heard their hearts, it was clear that God already had his people in place. It took them a little while to get used to the idea that they were the called ones, but gradually they took a deeply personal journey to the point where they could accept the challenge with a whole heart.

They had very little training, just a deep love for Bendigo and its young people and young mothers in particular. I can still remember the look of sheer terror mixed with a very small glimmer of excitement on Ian's face as it dawned on him that he might have to speak in public from time to time.

Ian and Jayne are still chook farmers, but they are chook farmers who have changed the lives of hundreds of people. The once vacant church is now a community centre. The youth work is largely overseen by young people who have come to faith and been discipled and trained through their ministry. A beautiful partnership has emerged with the local council to the point that when anyone wants to help people come together and celebrate, the council points them in the direction of the Dixons.

Ian and Jayne will be quick to tell you about their weaknesses, but the changed lives and the team that has grown around them will tell you about their faithfulness and their commitment. Ian and Jayne are platform builders.

Erion is another platform builder. He was only fourteen when the Albanian government fell and the madness started. Very quickly those people who had been regular church attenders read the new political reality and gave up their commitment to their faith. Some adults knocked on Erion's door and said, "Here are the keys to the church, it's all yours". It was a bewildering time for a young man who saw all the adults he had looked up to quickly renounce what they had been so publically proclaiming only weeks earlier.

Erion knew he couldn't and wouldn't give up. He called a meeting of the youth group and for a while they were all there was of that church. He loved Albania, and loved this Jesus he had only relatively recently discovered. That moment of commitment, of not giving up, laid a foundation for the direction his life was to take.

A little team of young people from Erion's youth group, and one other local church, committed themselves to bringing the Kingdom of God to their nation.

That was six years ago. It's not an easy journey in a majority Muslim country with significant poverty and corruption, but each year more and more young people are discovering faith and setting about changing the world.

One of the initiatives the team has taken has been to stage theatrical musical productions. Hundreds turn out to watch the productions, from communities across southern Albania that have rarely seen such a thing. Young people create the sets, rehearse the lines and have found their voices in performing Les Miserables, The Hunchback of Notre Dame and Oliver Twist.

The team run regular day trips for over 100 young people at a time, and the festivals they run across southern Albania draw communities together in ways that have never happened before.

If you talk to Erion or his offsiders Lorena and Lysenia about the remarkable work they are doing (in partnership with the local church), they will be quick to point out the weaknesses and gaps. However, if you talk to any of the hundreds of young people who have had their lives changed and who are finding their own places in ministry, you will quickly see what a difference a small group of friends can make in creating platforms for literally hundreds of others.

So what does it mean to be a platform builder?

As the diagram indicates, people are empowered as they are drawn into the heart of a Kingdom Cell. True empowerment happens as people discover their own relationship with Christ, accept a mission, find fellowship and begin to create platforms for others. The challenge of this though, is that they need to discover <u>their</u> relationship with Christ, <u>their</u> mission, fellowship that is real for <u>them</u>, what it means for <u>them</u> to be hospitable and how <u>they</u> empower others. One of our major limitations as human beings is that we can only see the world from where we are standing, and in our experience we are the centre of the universe. Most of our prayers and our evaluation of success or failure is limited by this.

To empower others we need to get some perspective. Towards the end of his time in the leadership of Fusion, my father kept saying "It's not what you do with your life, but what you set in motion that counts." The quote has stayed with me as I have watched Fusion's work grow around the world, knowing that it all started with the commitment of one teenager. Reinhold Niebuhr said "Nothing worth doing can be achieved in a lifetime."[171] The measure of success for us is not what we do; it is what is left after we are done, and most of that is about God's work and not ours!

Jesus addressed our tendency to become self-centred with the story of the growing seed: "This is what the kingdom of God is like. A man scatters seed on the ground. Night and day, whether he sleeps or gets up, the seed sprouts and grows, though he does not know how. All by itself the soil produces grain—first the stalk, then the head, then the full kernel in the head. As soon as the grain is ripe, he puts the sickle to it, because the harvest has come."[172] The farmer, who normally gets the credit for a crop, has the fairly simple task of spreading the seed; the work that produced the crop was done by the soil. This is what it means to be an agent of the Kingdom of God. You might have the opportunity to plant some seeds, but it is actually God that does the work. For those of us who have a tendency towards delusions of grandeur, this is a very important parable.

17

It's the Heart that Matters

As we truly open ourselves to Christ and the mission he gives us, we will also be opening ourselves to a dilemma: the mission he gives us is impossible. Whether it is raising children, running a business, abolishing slavery or struggling to get through the day with a broken body, God never calls us to a mission that we comfortably believe we can manage within the framework of our own resources. Seeking first the Kingdom of God requires dependence on God and interdependence with others. Dependence on God is hard enough, but interdependence with others can feel almost impossible.

I sometimes wonder how Jesus felt when he saw the gap between what he was able to do personally and what was needed. Matthew records that he saw the crowds and had "compassion on them, because they were harassed and helpless, like sheep without a shepherd."[173] His response was to say to the disciples "The harvest is plentiful but the workers are few. Ask the Lord of the harvest, therefore, to send out workers into his harvest field." Even the Son of God knew that he could not do all that was needed, that others would need to find their mission in the Kingdom if it were to become a reality.

If you were picking a group of people to change the world, do you think you would choose the twelve disciples? *The Message* paraphrase links the prayer at the end of Matthew chapter 9 to the choosing of the disciples: "The prayer was no sooner prayed than it was answered. Jesus called twelve of his followers and sent them into the ripe fields. He gave them power to kick out the evil spirits and to tenderly care for the bruised and hurt lives."[174] In choosing the twelve, Jesus was demonstrating how people get picked to work in the Kingdom of God. None of them seemed to come from the right schools or had the right accreditations within the religious system of the day. They were rough, and not always so bright. Even those who would end up as leaders kept making monumental mistakes, yet in the end, the chosen twelve (except Judas) became the foundation of the New Testament Church. Jesus cared about people's hearts and left the details to God.

We catch a further glimpse of what is important to God in the story of how a shepherd boy was chosen to be Israel's greatest king. David was the little guy that everyone forgot. His predecessor, Saul, was the biggest, strongest and smartest kid in the class. When Samuel went to anoint the new King, he met David's older brother who looked like a natural for the job, but God made clear that the way he makes decisions about people is not the way the world does: "Do not consider his appearance or his height, for I have rejected him. The Lord does not look at the things people look at. People look at the outward appearance, but the Lord looks at the heart."[175]

Latin American theologian Samuel Escobar caused quite a stir in 1999 with a paper he wrote claimed that the Western Christian church has fallen into what he called *managerial missiology*. What he meant by that was that somehow we have developed the belief that "missions can be approached like a business problem. With the right inputs, the thinking goes, the right outcomes can be assured."[176] By putting emphasis on inputs and outcomes we limit our ability to engage with the Kingdom to those things that we can see and measure, and we are in danger of measuring success in the way the world measures success.

In the last week before the crucifixion, Jesus took the disciples to the temple and sat up the back watching what was going on.[177] At one point he gestures to a fat, wealthy man and says something like, "Can you see how he is making a show of giving so much money to the temple? It's actually not costing him anything and that's just what it's worth to God!" He then points to a small, weathered, obviously poor and probably scruffy, old lady, "Can you see the couple of coins she is giving, those cost her everything, and that's what they are worth to God!" Jesus changed the game. Instead of tallying the outcome, he asked what the gift cost the giver.

It seems that while we tend to judge each other based on outcomes, God uses a different scale of measurement. He wants to know where a person's heart is, rather than how successful they appear, how much money they have or how many people listen to what they have to say. The Kingdom of God is not about how things appear, but about who people actually are. The most important criteria in the Kingdom of God is your heart, not your education, not your family, not your bank balance and not even how good or naughty you have been. The reason Jesus chose the disciples, the reason that God chose David, was because the foundation of who they were as people, their will, was open to God and his will.

Empowerment in the Kingdom of God is not about helping people become successful in the world's eyes, it is about creating a platform for them to fulfil the purpose God has for them.

Why and not what

Part of the realisation that is required of those who want to seek first the Kingdom of God, is that what they actually do, is far less important than why they do it. We need to start to face our own motivations.

We all harbour fantasies about the kind of things that would help us feel better about ourselves. Usually those fantasies come from our damaged self-esteem, and following them leads to disappointment. Dietrich Bonhoeffer wrote: "He who loves community, destroys community; he who loves the brethren, builds community."[178] Bonhoeffer is pointing out that the person who loves the idea of community will never be a community builder, because communities are made up of people and people are much more than any idea you might have. The only way to build community is to love people, not love community.

I have come to see that Bonheoffer's principle can be translated quite broadly. It can apply to plans we might have for a new building or a new organisation: the person who loves a new building or new organisation destroys them; he who loves the people who will be served by the building or organisation, builds the effectiveness of the building or organisation. It can apply to relationships: the person who loves the idea of marriage, destroys the marriage; the person who loves another, builds a marriage. The person who loves being a parent, destroys their children, it is the person who loves the children who is a great parent. It can also apply to roles: the person who wants to be a leader destroys their followers, but the person who loves the mission to which they are called and the people in their care, is a leader. The person who loves being a youth worker destroys young people; it is the person who loves the young people that makes an effective youth worker. The person who wants to be businessman may destroy a business: the person who loves their customers builds a business. I have seen this principle in operation over and over again, and I've learned to trust people who work towards a goal to be achieved, rather than those who focus on the particular role or action.

Because of the extent to which we all get easily seduced into looking for things to make us feel better about ourselves, empowerment is not always about saying yes. Paul exhorts Timothy in 1 Timothy 5:22, to "not be hasty in the laying on of hands." Just because somebody wants influence does not mean it is right. It is tempting to look for people's approval by telling them what their ego wants to hear and encouraging their fantasies. This approach never ends well. <u>Every time</u> I have encouraged someone to make a choice, which in retrospect was based on a fantasy, they lost heart and were out of ministry within 18 months.

There is a big difference between a fantasy and a mission. If you are called to a mission, you need to be willing to do any role, particularly the ones that give very little benefit to your ego. One story particularly stands out for me was that of a rich lady who was attracted to the idea of being a nun with Mother Teresa. Against her family's will, she went. She loved the idea of serving the poor. They gave her the job of cleaning the toilets. Apparently the toilets were really stomach turningly disgusting. As she went to clean these toilets, the rich young lady began dry retching. She found an alcove and cried and cried. Then she heard a noise in the hallway, a shuffling. She saw a little old nun cleaning the toilet and it only took half a second to realise who it was: Mother Theresa actually liked to clean toilets. The rich young woman never forgot that moment.

In his study of what makes good companies become great companies, Jim Collins concludes that the key is actually a servant leader, who is not so concerned with the leadership role or their own advancement. He labels this the "Level 5 leader." Collins says "Level 5 leaders channel their ego needs away from themselves and into the larger goal of building a great company. It's not that level 5 leaders have no ego or self-interest. Indeed they are incredibly ambitious – but *their ambition is first and foremost for the institution, not themselves.*"[179] There is nothing wrong with choosing a career path, in learning to be a writer, a youthworker, radio announcer or teacher, but in whatever role you find yourself you must face the fundamental question: "Is it about me, or is it about the Kingdom of God?"

The place of true empowerment is the place of humility and trust. Eugene Peterson says "The more we get involved in what God is doing, the less we find ourselves running things; the more we participate in God's work as revealed in Jesus, the more is done to us and the more is done through us."[180] This place requires us to face the things in ourselves that result in our own disempowerment, that want to take us away from our own platform, and as we do that we can help others face the things that take them away from their platform.

Empowerment means measuring your success not on your own actions, but on how you create the platform for others to fulfil their potential. It is highly likely that when Christ finally returns we will discover that some of the most effective Kingdom builders have been people we have never heard of, simply because they spent their whole lives creating platforms for others rather than seeking the limelight for themselves.

18

The Sixth Radical Decision: Commitment

Nik was a handful.

His father died while he was a baby and his mother couldn't look after him so he grew up with his very religious grandparents. At the age of four he became a Christian, but by the time he got to school he took the view that rules were there to be broken, and he broke them. His loud manner and demanding attitude meant he became an outsider amongst his classmates and was the victim of merciless bullying. After a couple of years he began to take his faith more seriously and began having deep discussions with some of his fellow students.

He and four other friends decided to form a group called "Slaves of Virtue" that was about committing to living a life of faith, and not just talking about it. They met regularly, read the Bible together and held one another accountable for their actions. When school eventually finished, their commitment remained. The small group of friends took on a new name, the "Order of the Mustard Seed", and focussed their mission on three commitments:

1. Be kind to all men
2. To be true to Christ
3. To send the gospel to the world.

Author Phil Anderson, who researched the life of Nikolaus Ludwig Zinzendorf (Nik), writes "To the members of the Order of the Mustard Seed, every follower of Christ was a missionary, whether at home, or in the farthest corners of the earth."[181] Nik and his friends committed their lives to changing the world because of their love for Christ and Anderson writes, "Zinzendorf's impact on history has been profound. His legacy has shaped the lives of people groups from the British to the Mohican Indians, the Afro-Caribbeans and the Greenland Eskimos. His influence has touched personalities as diverse as William Carey, Dietrich Bonhoeffer and Nelson Mandela."

Nik Zinzendorf's main legacy was his leadership of the Moravian community. The Moravians were widely regarded as second class citizens, moved on from town to town, until they met Nikolaus, who invited them to settle on his land. The community started to fragment after a bitter dispute, which Zinzendorf tried in vain to address. It wasn't until he discovered a dusty old book spelling out the heart and the history of the Moravians[182] that things really started to change. In the book he recognised the same longings and commitment that had driven him at school, and as he came home and shared the truths again of real faith with the community, things changed dramatically. The group met to pray and face the seriousness of their situation; they found themselves confessing their sins to each other and refocusing on Jesus. They committed to living faith in a real way, and committed to prayer. This remarkable little movement began sending missionaries all over the world, well before William Carey rediscovered the place of missions over 100 years later. It was this little group that had such a profound impact on John Wesley, on his trip home from America.

Zinzendorf showed with his life how significant commitment can be when it is placed in the context of a living relationship with Jesus, a mission and true fellowship.

The central difference between those who have changed the world with Jesus and those who haven't is commitment. The first and by far the most important commitment, is our commitment to God and his Son, Jesus Christ. From that main commitment, *commitment* to a mission, *commitment* to fellowship, *commitment* to hospitality and commitment to empowering others, are the foundations that produce a Kingdom Cell.

In a world of fast food, easy credit and a spiralling divorce rate, commitment seems a bit old fashioned. Bob Dylan sang, "The times they are a changing." In the second decade of the twenty first century, it's not only the times that are a changing, but everything, all the time.

Australian social researcher, Hugh Mackay, says the current generation of under 30's has learned to postpone long-term commitments in favour of short-term goals and temporary solutions. He says "Growing up in a world of ever-expanding choices, they have made a virtue of keeping their options open, and they have adopted *what else is there?* as their general catchcry. It's a question that comes up whether the topic is a course of study, a job, a sexual partner, a musical genre, an outing, a set of religious or political beliefs, a fashion label, a food fad or a make of car."[183]

Sure we want to change the world, but only if we can do it by lunchtime. Unfortunately, not a lot of world changing happens in that timeframe.

Social anthropologist, Margaret Mead, said "Never doubt that a small group of thoughtful, *committed* citizens can change the world; indeed, it's the only thing that ever has."[184] We in the church have become experts in organising events and running programs, but events and programs don't bring the Kingdom of God to earth, commitment does.

Jesus calls us out of our comfortable normality into the complexity of the real world. It took the greatest leader who ever lived three years to select, train and equip his disciples. Too often the Christian church has put a flurry of activity into a particular place or program, only to have it dissipate quickly. Proverbs 13:12 says *"Hope deferred makes the heart sick,"* and often we have been guilty of creating and then dashing hope because we're not prepared to stick with people and see things through.

Throughout the history of the church, those who have been willing to commit are the ones who have been used by God to bring transformation. One of the world's most respected management and leadership authors, Peter Drucker, wrote "Unless commitment is made, there are only promises and hopes; but no plans."[185]

I remember the moment I personally discovered the importance of commitment. I had just finished Fusion's six month intensive mission training course and was doing a six month placement in Hobart, Tasmania. Fusion's work in Tasmania had been through a challenging patch of time after the main leader had left to work in another state two years previously. I came fresh out of the training with lots of good ideas and not much else. I was terribly lonely, disillusioned and wondering whether God was actually there. All the things I thought seemed so easy in a classroom now seemed so complicated in real life. I kept looking for someone to tell me what to do, but no one seemed to know.

Our little team went to the home of an older friend and former Fusion worker's house for Sunday lunch and the conversation turned to Fusion in Tasmania. I remember clearly his words, "People have been coming and going from the team here in Hobart for too long, what it really needs is someone to dig in and commit." I remember the sick feeling in my stomach as I knew in my heart God was saying "Matt, that's you." I wrestled for a week but eventually gave in. I drove to the top of Mt. Wellington, which towers over the small city, and prayed, "OK God, you've got me; I'm willing to accept the challenge of this city."

That moment of commitment changed how I viewed my time in Hobart. I continued to make mistakes, lots of them, but they became points of learning as I continued to grow. I found myself more able to be creative, because I was now working towards a vision I carried rather than looking to others for direction. By the time I eventually left Australia's southernmost

State eleven years ago, I hadn't started a national movement, abolished slavery or become a national hero, but I had made a difference.

As I look back on that time, I am most proud of the team of people who grew around me, many of whom are continuing in leadership and ministry in other places. Together we ministered to thousands of young people, trained hundreds of Christians in effective mission, supported churches to come together in united witness, established a unique partnership with a municipal council to deliver services to young people and began an approach to training and working with at-risk young people in schools that resulted in us acquiring a farm and adventure based training facility.

Something happens when you commit. Suddenly you approach life in a different way. You are no longer waiting to be told what to do. You find a way. Management writer, John Maxwell, said: "Until I am committed, there is a hesitancy, a chance to draw back. But the moment I definitely commit myself, then God moves also, and a whole stream of events erupts. All manner of unforeseen incidents, meetings, persons, and material assistance, which I could never have dreamed would come my way, begin to flow toward me - the moment I make a commitment."[186]

Commitment comes at a price and a willingness to pay that price is not 'normal'. We live in a world that tells us to trust our feelings and to move towards things that give us pleasure and away from things that cause us pain. If you are not ready to commit, you are not on your own, the world is full of people floating around on the wind of circumstance. Unfortunately though, reading this book will have been a waste of time. The central thesis of this book is that the life of a Kingdom Cell comes through commitment. It comes through one main commitment, to Jesus, and four subsequent commitments that flow out of that first and main one.

There is nothing I can write, nothing anyone can say that will produce commitment in another person. It is always an individual choice but it is the most important choice of your life. George Lucas, writer and director of Star Wars, said: "You have to find something that you love enough to be able to take risks, jump over the hurdles and break through the brick walls that are always going to be placed in front of you. If you don't have that kind of feeling for what it is you are doing, you'll stop at the first giant hurdle."[187] This book is for people who are ready to jump over hurdles and break through brick walls.

The people I have mentioned in this book were people just like you and me. They also had moments when they just wanted to give up. The reason Jesus so dramatically defeated the forces of evil was that when everything in him wanted to give up, he held on and said, "Yet not as I will, but as you will."[188]

For most of the people I have written about we have at least some reference to their personal Gethsemanes; for others we can safely assume those moments were there.

There is a temptation to pretend people who change the world are somehow more than human. It's safer that way because it asks less of us. They weren't. They were simply committed. The world changed because of their commitment, and their lives ask each one of us one very simple question: *What are you willing to commit to?*

19

So What Now?

For too long we have tried to be distinctive by adapting our worship services and church structures, and tried to blend as best we could with the world we encounter from Monday to Saturday. It is time to stop blending.

Australian author, Mark Sayers wrote "One of the reasons the early church grew at such a phenomenal rate was that the lives of the early Christians spoke so strongly to their neighbours. There was something different about them, something that spoke of a different reality, an alternative way of living, to the culture around them. The early Christians lived lives of holiness that drew others to them and their life giving message."[189] We need to discover again what it means to be a Christ follower in the context of a complex and messy world, so that our distinctiveness might again stand out in the same way the early church's did.

N.T. Wright believes that Jesus intentionally formed "cells of followers, mostly continuing to live in their towns and villages, who by their adoption of his praxis, his way of being Israel, would be distinctive within their local communities."[190]

The Kingdom of God on earth is built by a movement of people who are distinctive within their local communities. The Kingdom of God comes to earth through ordinary people who live in a way so marked by the glory of God, because of their love for Jesus, that they stand out from the crowd. They demonstrate simply by the way they live, that there is a different way of being human than "normal." These people live distinctively within the sphere of society in which they find themselves. They run businesses distinctively, do art distinctively, parent distinctively, write computer programs distinctively, teach distinctively, build distinctively, suffer distinctively, and love distinctively. They may not use the terminology, and may not even have reflected on it, but as you speak with them you will discover that there are 6 radical decisions that make up the foundation of their lives.

1. Their relationship with Jesus is their main anchor point and the source of their motivation.

2. They have a mission that they are clearly working to wards most days of their life. Sometimes that mission will be grand, sometimes it will be simple, but in all cases it will change the world.

3. They value fellowship deeply and will tell you about the people whose friendship has helped them hold the course.

4. They are open and welcoming of new people and are fascinated by how different we all are. They will usually be able to tell you stories of fascinating people they have met, and many of those will not be the people society regards as rich or famous.

5. They are genuinely excited when other people make gains in the Kingdom of God, and will tell you about those they have helped along the way with a sense of pride.

6.   They will readily recount numerous times when they came close to giving up, but their commitment meant that they held on.

Imagine what would happen if everyone in the world knew someone like this?

Imagine if in every big corporate headquarters there were two or three Christ followers who had made glorifying God in that place, their ministry. Imagine what could happen if just one senior executive saw their ministry in a similar way. Imagine what could happen.

Imagine if in every school there were a two or three teachers who had made the six radical decisions and were forces for love and justice amongst both the staff and student body? Imagine what could happen if there were five or six students who saw bringing the Kingdom of God to earth in their school as the focus of their ministry? Imagine if a small group of parents saw their ministry as loving the students and staff of that school and working to bring God's glory in that place. Imagine what could happen.

Imagine if in every hospital there were patients who saw the way they managed their personal suffering as their personal ministry. Imagine if a handful of nurses saw their jobs as their ministry, and worked to bring love and justice to the patients in their care. Imagine if a couple of doctors and perhaps one hospital administrator also saw their ministries in this way. Imagine what could happen.

Imagine if in every community, in every suburb or village there were just two or three who accepted the burden of a ministry to bring the Kingdom of God in that place. Imagine if just one or two local councilors also saw their job as bringing love and justice to the community and three or four small business owners saw their businesses as ministry. Imagine what could happen.

Now imagine a local congregation where all of these people came together.

The C.E.O. might not fully understand what life is like for the patient, and the student might not fully understand what life is like for the politician, but together they are a family. Worship would continually re-focus them, teaching would equip them to make sense of themselves and the world, prayer would carry them and fellowship would encourage and sustain them. This is how it is meant to be: Christ's followers expressing their discipleship through two structures in the body, the Kingdom Cell and the congregation. It is this inter-relation of both structures that is the picture of the body of Christ at its best.

Our world is hungry for hope. It is not looking for a new theory but people who can show a way forward, amidst the chaos of conflicting voices. We are called to live lives that stand out clearly against the backdrop of the world as a model of a different way. This is our task. As you come to the end of this book, my sincere hope is that you have caught a glimpse of how possible this task actually is.

I hope that you have been challenged to be more open to a real relationship with Jesus.

I hope that you have a sense of the mission Jesus is inviting you to take on, even if it's not a grand plan yet, and that you can see where you can make a start.

I hope you can see what you can do to find the fellowship you need on the journey.

I hope you are starting to see the people God is asking you to love and be hospitable to.

I hope you are seeing what it means to empower those around you, and that you have been challenged to pick up your particular cross in order for that to happen.

I hope you might be at a point where you are ready to commit.

There are now 6 radical choices that are in front of you: make them, and the world will change.

Discussion Guide for Small Groups

$\mathbf{T}$he following discussion guide is designed for small groups of between 3 and 12 to share together on a weekly basis for seven weeks.

This book is not designed to be just another theological theory, but a call to action. My hope is that by discussing the issues raised with a group of people, some of the challenges contained in the book will be focussed more sharply and that God might deepen your awareness of yourself, Him and others.

Some helpful points

- I would encourage you to open each session in prayer, and close in prayer. As I say on each session, Satan has an investment in you not taking this material too seriously and my guess is that he will try hard to divert you.

- The Bible readings will be most useful if they are read from a couple of different translations (often the Message puts things in a helpful way), and there is space to discuss and respond to the readings before moving on.

- The questions are designed to be a little bit confronting, to help you move information from your head to your heart. If they are not working for your group, you might find another way to engage with the material.

- Be as honest as you can be, the more deeply you are able to share, the more deeply God will be able to speak through you to others and through others to you.

- In the 'sharing for prayer', it will really help if you can be as specific with what you need prayer for as possible, so the whole group can watch and see how God responds.

More questions, resources, and a study leaders guide are available for free at **www.kingdomcells.org**

Session One: Jesus

Share:

What would you hope to gain personally from engaging with this book? What would you like to see in your group as a result of engaging with 6 Radical Decisions?

Read:

2 Corinthians 5:14-21

Discuss:

- Are there times when you tend to lose sight of Jesus? What are the settings this is most likely to happen?

- If seeking first God's Kingdom means his will in every area of your life, what does that mean for you? Are there any areas of your life where you know that he is not in charge? What areas of your life would he want to talk to you about? What would he want to say?

- Bill Bright responded with tears at the question of what Jesus meant for him. Have there been times when your relationship with Jesus has been like that? What was happening at the time?

- Close your eyes and picture yourself at the foot of the cross looking into the eyes of Jesus. What does your heart sense that he might want to say to you?

Pray:

Share with each other how your life would need to change for your relationship with Jesus to become deeper and more real. Pray for each other. Pray for protection for the group. Satan doesn't want you to love Jesus more deeply.

Session Two: Mission

Share:

Where have you seen Jesus in the last week?

Read:

John 20:19-21. Imagine you were one of the disciples. How would you be feeling before Jesus appeared? How would you be feeling after?

Discuss:

- God's glory is his nature, his justice and love. We are called to glorify God by making his nature manifest on earth. What are the injustices that you would most like to see change? What people can you see in your network of relationships, most need to be loved?

- Ephesians 2:10 says "For we are God's handiwork, created in Christ Jesus to do good works, which God prepared in advance for us to do." Do you have a sense of the work that God has prepared for you to do? Even if it's not absolutely clear, describe to the group your understanding of what God is asking of you.

- N.T. Wright said "Your task is to find the symbolic ways of doing things differently, planting flags in hostile soil, setting up signposts that say there is a different way to be human." In what ways might you act symbolically, even in a small way, to bring the Kingdom of God? Agree together what action you will each take in the coming week.

Pray:

Pray for each other as you contemplate what it means to put your faith into action. Pray for the protection of the Group. Satan doesn't want you discovering and living your God-given purpose.

Session Three: Fellowship

Share:
How has your relationship with Jesus been over the past week?
What have you done to move forward on the mission God has given you?

Read:
Philippians 2:1-18

Discuss:

- What are the relationships in your life that you are committed to? List them and share them. What does the list tell you about yourself?

- Have there been times when fellowship has made a real difference for you? Share and discuss what you learned from that experience.

- Write down a list of people you would say really know what life is like for you. Write another list of people you would say that you know well enough to know what life is like for them. Discuss what those lists tell you about the current level of fellowship you are having.

- Paul talks about a thorn in the flesh. Do you know what yours is? How do you manage it? Share to the level you feel able.

Pray:
Share what you sense God wants you to do about strengthening the level of fellowship you have. Pray for each other.
Pray for the protection of the group. Satan has an investment in keeping you isolated.

Session Four: Hospitality

Share:

How has your relationship with Jesus been over the past week?
What have you done to move forward on the mission God has given you?
How have you experienced fellowship in the last week?

Read:

Isaiah 54:2-5

Discuss:

- How do you feel about 'extending the place of your tent' and welcoming people into your life? Have there been times where hospitality has brought you joy? Share them. Have there been times where hospitality has brought you pain? Share those too.

- How ready are you to be hospitable? How much time is available in your calendar? How much room is available in your home? How much space is available in your heart? Share what making the space for hospitality would mean for you.

- As an assignment this week choose to spend time with someone who doesn't think or act like you at all, someone you wouldn't normally spend time with. Genuinely make space for them. Share who that person is with the group and next week be ready to share what happened.

Pray:

Share with the group what in your life needs to change in order for you to be more hospitable. Pray for each other. Pray for the protection of the group. Satan doesn't want you affecting others.

Session Five: Empowerment

Share:
How did spending time with the person who was different to you go?
How has your relationship with Jesus been over the past week?
What have you done to move forward on the mission God has given you?
How have you experienced fellowship in the last week?

Read:
Acts 11:19-30

Discuss:

• Who are the people that have built a platform for you?
Share with the group what they did that made
a difference.

• Have you ever felt disempowered? Share with the group
how it happened and what it felt like.

• Are there people with potential, like Saul, around you
who need someone to see them and encourage them?
If you can see them, what will you do about that?
If you can't see them, what does that tell you about
yourself?

• Are there other churches or groups near you? Discuss
what you can do as a group to encourage and
empower them.

Pray:
Share with the group how God is asking you to empower the people around
you. Pray for each other.
Pray for protection for the group. The last thing Satan wants are more
people becoming empowered to be the people God created them to be.

Session Six: Commitment

Share:

How has your relationship with Jesus been over the past week?

What have you done to move forward on the mission God has given you?

How have you experienced fellowship in the last week?

How have you been hospitable in the last week? What was it like?

How have you encouraged and empowered others? What was the result?

Read:

The story of Jesus in the Garden of Gethsemane. (Matthew 26:36-25)

Discuss:

- Have you ever been at a point where it seemed everything in you wanted to take an easier option, but you knew the right choice to make? Describe the situation and what eventually happened.

- Romans 5 indicates that hope comes as a result of persevering in the face of suffering. What are the things you need to persevere with at the moment?

- What do you sense would need to change in your life for you to be able to say with integrity that you are committed to Christ, to a mission, to fellowship, to hospitality and to empowerment? Be specific.

- What do you believe God is asking you to actually commit to? Will you?

Pray:

Share what it is you believe it is right to be committed to.

Pray that God would bless that commitment and would grant you the courage to hang on to it when it's not easy. Pray that God would protect the group. Satan doesn't want you to be committed to anything but your own feelings, because he can manipulate them.

Session Seven: What's next?

Share:

How has your relationship with Jesus been over the past week?

What have you done to move forward on the mission God has given you?

How have you experienced fellowship in the last week?

How have you been hospitable in the last week? What was it like?

How have you encouraged and empowered others? What was the result?

Read:

Ephesians 4:1-16

Discuss:

- Paul talks about Apostles, Prophets, Evangelists and Pastor/Teachers doing their work so that we might become mature and not tossed around by life. Can you see the areas you still need to become more mature in? If so, share them. If not, do you have the courage to ask the group what they see in you?

- What is the mission God has called you to? Who do you know that is called to a similar mission?

- What would you need to do to start a Kingdom Cell made up of people who are called to a similar mission to you? What benefits can you see to this? What would be the challenges? What are you going to do about it?

- If it's not yet clear what mission God has called you to, what could you do in order to bring the Kingdom to your neighbourhood? Who else might join you in the challenge? What are you going to do about it?

- What congregation are you committed to?
What can you do to strengthen your relationship
with that congregation?

- What has God shown you over the last seven weeks
of engagement with this book? How would your
life change if you were to take them seriously?
Be specific.

Pray:

Share what you sense God is asking you in relation to being part of a
Kingdom Cell.

Share what you would like to change in your life as a result of engaging with
this book.

Share what you know you will need people to keep praying for you for if
you are to make the choices God is asking you to make. Pray for each other.
Pray also for the protection of the group. Satan is scared.

Foundations for Life and Mission

If you are ready to face the challenge of the five commitments of the Kingdom Cell, there is no course I know better able to equip you to face the real questions you will need to face than Foundations for Life and Mission.

At a student of the Foundations for Life and Mission one week short course you will:

- Move towards a free and loving relationship with Jesus through a deep engagement with the word of God.
- Come to a deeper understanding of the particular plan God has for your life.
- Discover a fresh appreciation of the wonderful complexity of humanity and how aspects of your humanity that can hold you back from becoming all you, and others, are created to be.
- Develop the skills, knowledge and awareness necessary to be more effective in empowering others and engaging in real fellowship and hospitality.

Foundations courses are held all over the world. If you would like more information about courses near you, or would like to organise a course in your city, contact office@fusionyac.org

Connect with Others on the Journey

A partnership of people around the world have committed themselves to doing whatever we can to support those who are ready to accept the challenge of the 6 Radical Decisions of the Kingdom Cell.

We have established a website (**www.kingdomcells.org**) that we hope will be a place where those who are wrestling with what it means to actually live the Kingdom can share experiences and resources. The site also has a page of resources for churches interested in using this book as a focus for their small groups. (You can also register on the website to be informed about new resources as they become available.)

A twitter feed (@**kingdomcells**) is another way to continue the conversation. Let us know how you found the book and stay in touch with what Kingdom Cells around the world are up to.

End Notes

1 Matthew 6:33

2 The notion of the "Kingdom of God" is actually quite simple. The English word "kingdom" comes from the words "King's Dominion" or "where the King rules". Stanley J. Grenz, Theology for the Community of God (1994), 476 says the Kingdom of God "is a reality that people can enter (Mark 9:47; Matt 21:31-32), for it is the kingly power of God. Hence, the kingdom is a "sphere of existence" in which people are called to live."

3 https://www.cia.gov/library/publications/the-world-factbook/geos/xx.html

4 Richard Eckersley, Well and Good (2005), 7

5 These statistics are primarily from America.Ronald J. Sider, The Scandal of Evangelical Conscience (2005),13,21,24,27

6 Matthew 7:20

7 As quoted by Charlie Webster, Revitalising Christianity (2011),207

8 I've borrowed this explanation of our task from N.T. Wright in his book Surprised by Hope (2008),204

9 Stanley J. Grenz, Theology for the Community of God (1994), 476

10 M. Scott Peck, The Different Drum (1987),25

11 Mark Foreman, Wholly Jesus: His Surprising Approach to Wholeness and Why It Matters Today (2008), 91

12 Matthew 6:33

13 Galatians 6:2 "Carry each other's burdens". The Greek word for burden is baros in verse 2 signifies a load too big to be carried by one person, a heavy or crushing load. There are some loads which we need our brothers and sisters in Christ to carry with us, if we are not to be crushed. While the text is directly referencing the person who is caught in a sin being in need of fellowship, the principle can also be extended to other burdens.

14 Eugene Peterson, Christ Plays in Ten Thousand Places (2005), 117

15 Karl Barth, 'The Living Congregation of the Living Lord Jesus Christ', in Man's Disorder and God's Design. Volume 1: The Universal Church in God's Design, (1948), p. 73

16 Mark Greene, The Great Divide (2010),8

17 ibid

18 As quoted by Craig A. Carter in The community of the Word, toward an Evangelical Ecclesiology edited by Mark Husbands and Daniel J. Trier (2005), 186

19 In most English translations of the Bible, it appears that the gifts of Pastor and Teacher are separate, but in the original language it is clear that they are related, which makes sense. A pastor who can't teach produces dependency and a teacher who doesn't care produces alienation

20 Ephesians 4:12-13

21 Winter outlined this in an address that became a widely referenced paper entitled The two structures of God's redemptive mission. It has been reproduced many times but is currently part of the text Foundations of the World Christian Movement: A Larger Perspective (2008),227. His basic idea

continues to have fairly wide acceptance e.g. Howard A. Snyder, The community of the King (2004),173; Darrel L. Guder, The continuing conversion of the church (2000),182; Timothy C. Tennent, Invitation to World Missions: A Trinitarian Missiology for the Twenty-first Century(2010),439; Neil Cole, Organic Leadership: Leading Naturally Right Where you are (2010),122

[22] Ralph D. Winter, Foundations of the World Christian Movement A Larger Perspective (2008),229

[23] Ralph D. Winter, Foundations of the World Christian Movement A Larger Perspective (2008),229

[24] Fusion was originally called Teen Crusaders. The Fusion Website is www.fusioninternational.org

[25] Hugh Thomson Kerr, John M. Mulder, Famous conversions: the Christian experience (1983), 58

[26] John Wesley, Albert Cook Outler, John Wesley (1964), 66

[27] Pronounced Whitfield

[28] http://www.bbc.co.uk/humber/famous_folk/wesley/biography.shtml

[29] http://en.wikipedia.org/wiki/100_Greatest_Britons

[30] Donald Miller, Blue Like Jazz (2003), 233

[31] From Documentary film, Mother Theresa, As quoted by Ira Rifkin, Spiritual Leaders who changed the world (2008), 187

[32] Alan Hirsch, The Forgotten Ways (2006), 99

[33] Roger Thoman, Simple / House Church Revolution (2008), 14

[34] Matthew 13:18-23

[35] N.T. Wright Simply Christian (2006), 104

[36] John 14:6

[37] The Merriam-Webster dictionary says "Isms" are a distinctive doctrine, cause, or theory

[38] N.T. Wright, Calvin College Lecture series, (2002), Podcast (http://ntwrightpodcast.blogspot.com)

[39] As quoted by Stephen R. Covey, The Seven Habits of Highly Effective People (1990), 128

[40] Simon P. Walker, Leading out of who you are: Discovering the Secret of Undefended Leadership (2007), 158

[41] Jenny Garvin, The Journey – the History of Fusion International, (PDF document downloaded from www.lifeunderstanding.com)

[42] Charlotte Perkins Gilman, The living of Charlotte Perkins Gilman: an autobiography (1991), Page 42

[43] Eugene Peterson's The Message paraphrase of the Bible is the one I most often use for my personal reflections

[44] As quoted by Rick Warren, The Purpose Driven Life (2002),80

[45] Luke 9:23-25

[46] Galatians 2:7

[47] From Howard A. Snyder, The Radical Wesley and patterns for church Renewal (1980), 33

[48] From Dr. And Mrs. Howard Taylor, Hudson Taylor's Spiritual Secret (1990),8

[49] As quoted by George Scott Railton, The authoritative life of General William Booth (1912), 315

[50] From Sam Wellman, Mother Theresa Missionary of Charity (1997), 76

[51] Shane Claiborne, The Irresistible Revolution: Living as an Ordinary Radical (2006), 89

[52] 2 Corinthians 5:18-19

[53] Matthew Henry, The miscellaneous works of the Rev. Matthew Henry (1830), 419

[54] John 13:31

[55] Romans 3:23

[56] Colossians 1:27

[57] John 15:8

[58] Exodus 33:18

[59] Exodus 34:6-7

[60] As quoted by Stephen J.N. Nichols The Glory of God Present and Past, in The Glory of God (Kindle Edition) Edited by Christopher W. Morgan & Robert A. Peterson, (2010) Loc. 603

[61] Richard R. Melick Jr., The Glory of God in the Synoptic Gospels, Acts, and the General Epistles, in The Glory of God (Kindle Edition) Edited by Christopher W. Morgan & Robert A. Peterson, (2010) Loc. 1875

[62] John 19:30

[63] Robert S. Birchard, Cecil B. DeMille's Hollywood (2004)

[64] Christopher W. Morgan, Towards a Theology of the Glory of God The Glory of God (Kindle Edition) (2010), Location 3901

[65] Quoted in Elaine Murray Stone, Maximilian Kolbe: Saint of Auschwitz (1997), 80

[66] As quoted by Jennifer C. Jackson, Ethics in medicine (2006), 232

[67] I am indebted to N.T. Wright for this image

[68] John 20:21

[69] Twice in Matthew, once in Mark and twice in Luke

[70] in a sermon on the glory of God in 1843,

[71] E. Tucker, The Oberlin evangelist, Volume 5, Revelation of God's Glory, Sermon by Prof. Finney, (1843), 201

[72] John R. W. Stott, Sermon on the Mount (2000), 6

[73] Romans 3:23

[74] Loren Cunningham, Making Jesus Lord: The Dynamic Power of Laying Down Your Rights (1997), 134

[75] Stephen Tomkins, The Clapham Sect: How Wilberforce's circle changed Britain (2010), 1

[76] http://www.historyhome.co.uk/peel/religion/relig3.htm

[77] Mark Greene, The Great Divide (2010), 4

[78] Isaiah 8:18

[79] Check out streetlights.gr

[80] vimeo: https://vimeo.com/32315016

[81] http://www.bbc.co.uk/news/uk-scotland-17611036

[82] Acts 2:47

[83] Nelson Mandela, No easy walk to freedom (1973), 31

[84] Eddie Gibbs, Leadership Next (2005), 91

[85] Paulo Friere, Pedagogy of the Oppressed (1970), Chapter two

[86] Tremper Longman III, The Glory of God in the Old Testament, The Glory of God (Kindle Edition) Edited by Christopher W. Morgan & Robert (2010), Loc.1223

[87] Matthew 20:25-28

[88] Max Weber, The Theory of Social and Economic Organisation (1947)

[89] Eugene H. Peterson, Christ Plays in Ten Thousand Places (2005),272

[90] Max Weber, The Theory of Social and Economic Organisation (1947)

[91] http://www.orthodoxytoday.org/articles4/MotherTeresaAbortion.php

[92] Tony Campolo, Choose Love not Power (2009),121

End Notes

[93] http://news.bbc.co.uk/onthisday/hi/dates/stories/august/21/newsid_2534000/2534945.stm

[94] Your local church or organisations like Scripture Union, Share Jesus International and Fusion (the group I work with) are a good place to start.

[95] Tony Campolo, Choose Love not Power (2009),43

[96] Acts 17:16

[97] John 11:35

[98] St. Basil the Great, Epistle II (circa 358 A.D.) (accessed from www.ocf.org)

[99] Bruce Dutton, Bewdy Basil (On Being Magazine, September 1984), 43

[100] ibid

[101] Emphasis mine

[102] Pope Benedict, Address given July 4th 2007 and printed in the National Catholic Register, (July 15-21 2007)

[103] Duncan B. Forrester, The church as the servant of the new Europe (1994), published in Christian responsibility and the new Europe, University of Edinburgh, 15

[104] John 13:34-35

[105] I first heard my Father, Mal, use the same question many years ago, and the question remains as challenging for most of us now as it was then

[106] Howard A. Snyder, New Wineskins (1978),79

[107] Romans 12:15

[108] Alan Hirsch, The Forgotten Ways (2006), 221

[109] Alan Hirsch, The Forgotten Ways (2006), 224

[110] Article from Sydney Morning Herald 26 May 2010 Why you can count on your friends

[111] Dietrich Bonhoeffer, Life Together(1996),32

[112] Jean Vanier, Community and Growth (1989),25

[113] Tony Campolo, Choose Love not Power (2009),26

[114] James Lawrence, Growing Leaders (2004),238

[115] Eugene H. Peterseon, Christ plays in ten thousand places (2005),327

[116] John 13:34-35

[117] Romans 12:8

[118] J.Oswald Sanders, Spiritual Leadership (Second Revision) (1994),27

[119] As quoted by J. Oswald Sanders, Spiritual Leadership (Second Revision) (1994),118

[120] J.Oswald Sanders, Spiritual Leadership (Second Revision) (1994),118

[121] Matthew 26:37-40

[122] Jean Vanier, Community and Growth (1989),220

[123] The article appeared in Melbourne's Herald Sun on November 7th 2006

[124] 2 Corinthians 12:7-8

[125] Aaron Sorkin, West Wing Season 1, Episode 13, Take out the Trash Day (2000)

[126] ibid

[127] Eugene H. Peterseon, Christ plays in ten thousand places (2005),320

[128] Harold Myra and Marshall Shelley, The Leadership Secrets of Billy Graham (2005), 54

[129] Henri J.M. Nouwen, Reaching Out (1980),68

[130] ibid

[131] Henri J.M. Nouwen, Reaching Out (1980),91

[132] Henri J.M. Nouwen, Reaching Out (1980),52

[133] Marvin E. Shaw, Group dynamics, the psychology of small group behaviour (1971),104

[134] Henri J.M. Nouwen, Reaching Out (1980),91

[135]ibid

[136]1Peter 5:2-3 (The Message)

[137]Matt Garvin, Faith Reflections (2010),69-85

[138]Isaiah 54:2-3

[139]More information about Open Crowd Festivals is available at fusionyac.org

[140]Bono, on the move (2006), 16

[141]Richard Collier, The General Next to God (1968), 6

[142]Ronald J. Sider, The Scandal of Evangelical Conscience (2005), 119

[143]From The Message

[144]Nelson Mandela, Long Walk to freedom (1994),558

[145]Bartlett, Andrew. Entry points for Empowerment. CARE Bangladesh. (2004),

[146]Webster-Merriam dictionary

[147]Genesis 2:7

[148]Hebrew *ruah*, Greek *pneuma*

[149]As reported by Stanford News: http://news.stanford.edu/news/2005/june15/jobs-061505.html

[150]Peter Kreeft, Three Philosophies of Life (1989),20

[151]I believe the teacher was Solomon, the text clearly wants us to think that, but there is debate about the actual author.

[152]Mark 10:13-16, Luke 18:15-17

[153]Luke 18:17 and Mark 10:15

[154]Literal English Translation by Reverend Alfred Marshall in The Interlinear NIV parallel New Testament in Greek and English (1998),635

[155]Paulo Friere, Pedagogy of the Oppressed (1996),31

[156]Philippians 4:11-13

[157]Colossians 1:27

[158]Romans 7:15

[159]Romans 7:18-19

[160]Walt Kelly, The Best of Pogo, Edited by Mrs. Walt Kelly and Bill Crouch Jr. (1982),224

[161]Charles Bradley Templeton, Evangelism for Tomorrow (1957), 24 (He acknowledged that he was paraphrasing G.K. Chesterton)

[162] Matthew 18:6

[163] 1 Corinthians 10:32

[164]see Acts 11:19-24

[165]From The Message

[166]Acts 15:38

[167]2 Timothy 4:11

[168]http://www.bbc.co.uk/religion/religions/christianity/people/williamwilberforce_1.shtml

[169]Phil 2:3-4

[170]Greg Ogden, Daniel Meyer, Leadership Essentials: Shaping Vision, Multiplying Influence (2007),61

[171]Reinhold Niebuhr, quoted in Elizabeth Sifton, The Serenity Prayer: Faith and Politics in times of Peace and War (2003), 349

[172]Mark 4:26-29

[173]Matthew 9:36

[174]Matthew 10:1(The Message)

End Notes

[175] 1 Samuel 16:7

[176] Stan Guthrie Missions in the Third Millennium: 21 Key Trends for the 21st Century (2005), p192

[177] Mark 12:41-44

[178] Jean Vanier, Community and Growth (1989), 20

[179] Jim Collins, Good to Great (2001), 21

[180] Eugene H. Peterson, Christ plays in Ten Thousand places (2005), 231

[181] Phil Anderson, The Lord of The Ring (2007), 38

[182] Account of Discipline of the Brethren Church by Jan Amos Comenius

[183] Hugh Mackay. Advance Australia…Where? (2008) e-book edition

[184] Nancy Lutkehaus, Margaret Mead: the making of an American icon (2008), 261

[185] Peter F. Drucker, Management: tasks, responsibilities, practices (1974), 123

[186] http://globalchristiancentre.com/church-leadership/managing-maxwells-morale.html

[187] As quoted by Pat Williams, Michael Weinreb, How to be like Mike: life lessons about basketball's best (2001), 45

[188] Matthew 26:39

[189] Mark Sayers, The Vertical Self (2010), preface page xix

[190] N.T. Wright, Jesus and the Victory of God (1996), 276

Acknowledgements

I have been in ministry for 20 years and in many ways this book is a culmination of those twenty years. The many people I have worked with in Tasmania and Victoria as well as those with whom I have spent time with around Australia and the globe, have helped me see the heart of the material contained in this book. I wish I could name each one, but I think many will be able to read between the lines and see where particular understandings came from.

The Fusion team working on preparations for the London Olympics have been a real encouragement and this book simply wouldn't have been finished without them. Thanks so much Jenny, Dan, Dave, Claire, Andy, Skye, Craig and Gordon. I want to specially thank Marty who has both believed and pushed and pushed, so that now there actually is a book!

I am so grateful for my wife, Leeanne, who in 1994 agreed to take the ride of life as my partner and has shared both the incredible highs and desperate lows of that journey. She has been a real encouragement and support, and never stops believing in me. Also my children: Maddi, Josh, Dan and Sophie are a real joy and I am so thankful for each of them.

I have learned so much from my Dad both in listening to him and watching him that it is hard to know how to communicate my gratitude. I think I understand why Bono wrote "You're the reason why the opera is in me" to his father.

I am also deeply grateful for my mum who has made sure I knew I was loved from the day I was born. I have been inspired by the way she has held on to God in the last few years as things haven't been simple.

Acknowledgements

Auntie Anne is my first line of editorial support and one person cheer squad. I have been very grateful for her support and friendship and the regular cuppas with her and Mema.

I want to thank each of the people who took the time to read the manuscript at various phases of development and give very specific and helpful feedback. Thanks to Andy Frost, Jon Burns, Ruth Bushyager, Peter Corney, Dave Hammond, Rich Wilson, Jenny Woods and Tania Bright. Di Adams, particularly, went through a pile of A4 paper containing the seventh draft with a fine tooth comb and fixed most of the mistakes and tidied up my grammar. It wasn't a small job and I'm very grateful.

Thanks to my friend Heather (heatherbradbury.com) who turned a manuscript into a book and found a way to express the heart of the words into a look and feel.

Thanks too, to my editor Liza Hoeksma, who helped me see how much work I still needed to do, and as a result dramatically improved the book. I'm now a believer in editors!! Also thanks to Stephen Pillinger whose attention to detail made such a different to the end result.

I would also like to thank my Father and Mother in Law who have made a practise for many years of coming up to our house and quietly fixing many of the things that I wouldn't ever get to – or even know where to start with. Robert and Martry even created the little study that I am writing this book in. Their generosity of heart and hard work have made a big difference for me and Leeanne.

Finally I would like to thank the Fusion family, past and present, for creating the space for me to learn and grow, make mistakes and do a few useful things. This book has come out of a wrestle with how to do faith in a relevant way, the same wrestle which produced the Fusion movement.

Matt Garvin

As the son of the founder of the Evangelical Christian mission movement, Fusion, Matt Garvin grew up amongst people who had given their lives for the sake of the Gospel. Matt began work himself with Fusion in 1992 after completing a broadcast journalism cadetship in the Australian outback city of Broken Hill. In his time with Fusion, Matt has led Fusion's work in Tasmania and Victoria and lived in 5 different intentional Christian communities. He has also served in Fusion's international leadership and has had a continuing involvement in radio broadcasting in Australia. Matt travels around Australia and the world; training churches and individuals who are seeking to reach out to their communities. Matt is married to Leeanne and they have four children: Madeline, Joshua, Daniel and Sophie.

Also by Matt Garvin

Faith Reflections is an unusual book.

Most books start with a theme and a plan. This book started simply as a series of reflections on Matt's personal journey with faith on his blog faithreflections.org.

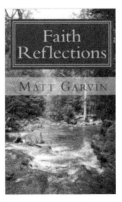

Most books have chapters; this book has a series of reflections that are loosely grouped thematically, but only loosely.

Matt says "I don't profess to be an expert on faith, and am very suspicious of anyone who does. I am simply a person on a journey. My prayer is that you might find this book at least a little bit helpful on your own journey."

"Almost without exception things never work out the way you imagine they might. What I can report though, is that if you are prepared to hold on and trust as best as you can, God can be trusted. I don't want to pretend that faith is easy. God always seems to lead me to a place that is outside my comfort zone and many times I make choices that are anything but faithful."

"For me faith is a real wrestle, which is why I am excited about this book. It is a chance to share the wrestle and explore this journey of faith."

Faith Reflections is available from most online booksellers